None Wounded,
None Missing, All Dead

None Wounded, None Missing, All Dead

The Story of Elizabeth Bacon Custer

Howard Kazanjian
Chris Enss

TWODOT®

GUILFORD, CONNECTICUT
HELENA, MONTANA
AN IMPRINT OF GLOBE PEQUOT PRESS

A · T W O D O T® · B O O K

Copyright © 2011 by Howard Kazanjian and Chris Enss

Text design: Sheryl P. Kober
Layout: Joanna Beyer

Library of Congress Cataloging-in-Publication Data
Kazanjian, Howard.
  None wounded, none missing, all dead : the story of Elizabeth Bacon Custer / Howard Kazanjian, Chris Enss.
    p. cm.
  Includes bibliographical references.
  ISBN 978-0-7627-5969-9
  1. Custer, Elizabeth Bacon, 1842-1933. 2. Custer, Elizabeth Bacon, 1842-1933—Marriage. 3. Custer, George A. (George Armstrong), 1839-1876. 4. Generals' spouses—United States—Biography. 5. Frontier and pioneer life—West (U.S.) 6. West (U.S.)—History—1860-1890—Biography. 7. Indians of North America—Wars—1866-1895. 8. Indians of North America—Wars—Great Plains. 9. United States. Army. Cavalry, 7th. I. Enss, Chris, 1961- II. Title.
  E467.1.C99K37 2011
  973.8'2092—dc22
  [B]

                                                                    2011000567

Printed in the United States of America

10 9 8 7 6 5 4 3 2 1

Contents

ACKNOWLEDGMENTS

During our time working on this book, we have become indebted to many people. We can only try to thank all of those who helped us along the way.

First must come Chris Kortlander, a gentleman who has offered his expertise and privately owned materials to make this tome unique. Mr. Kortlander is the director of the Custer Battlefield Museum in Garryowen, Montana, and is a walking encyclopedia on the subject of Elizabeth and George Custer. He has served as an indispensable "resource man," opening his archives and allowing us to use never-before-seen materials to complete this manuscript. He cherishes the items that once belonged to Elizabeth, including her wedding mementos, photographs, private letters, newspaper clippings, and travel journals. We appreciate his kindness and generosity.

Every biographer of a person of an earlier era owes much to the adequacy of libraries and the skill of librarians. We offer our appreciation to the West Point Library and staff; the Denver Public Library and its staff; the Detroit Public Library and its librarian and photo archivist, Ashley Koebel; the librarians at Yale University Library; and the staff at the Nevada County Library in Nevada City, California.

We were sent valuable material from archives in the State Historical Societies of Montana, Missouri, South Dakota, and Washington, D.C. We are grateful for their cooperation.

Thanks to Russ Ronspies with the Frontier Army Museum at Fort Leavenworth for providing information about the Custers' time in Kansas. Chief historian John Doerner of the Little Bighorn Battlefield National Monument deserves a note of thanks, as well.

We gained much from personal interviews and are appreciative of the time author Gail Kelly-Custer and former director of the Little Bighorn Battlefield National Monument Nadya Henry gave us. Thank you.

Finally, we are obliged to our editor, Erin Turner, and all those at Globe Pequot Press who brought this book into being.

INTRODUCTION

On June 27, 1876, Captain Frederick William Benteen spotted a cluster of white objects lying in a heap on a hill north of the Bighorn River in southern Montana. Benteen, a forty-two-year-old career army officer with a shock of white hair combed dramatically back over his long, bare forehead and harassed face, urged his horse slowly toward the knoll. A party of dutiful soldiers followed along behind him. As Captain Benteen inched his horse cautiously onto the site, it became clear that the achromatic objects lying motionless in the tall grass were the remains of General George Custer* and his regiment. The flesh and bones of 210 members of the 7th Cavalry lay strewn over a mile of bloody ground. All of the bodies except for General Custer's had been stripped naked and mutilated.[1]

Captain Benteen climbed down off his horse and made his way to General Custer's body, stepping over dead soldiers pierced by arrows and lances in the process. George Custer's ghostly frame was riddled with a number of injuries, not the least of which was a gunshot wound to the left

---

* At the time of the Battle of the Little Bighorn, George Armstrong Custer was a lieutenant colonel with the 7th U.S. Cavalry. During the Civil War, however, he had achieved the brevet (temporary) wartime rank of major general at the age of twenty-five, becoming famous as the "Boy General." The informal use of that rank followed him for the rest of his life and into the history books.

flank and left temple. Benteen studied the bodies around him, noticing that not only did the Indians in the fight leave George's remains intact, but they had also left his socks on his feet.* They had not scalped him, either, leaving his short, wavy hair undisturbed.[2]

"There he is, God damn him," Benteen said coldly to members of his battalion, busy digging graves to bury the dead. "He'll never fight anymore." Benteen had known the popular Boy General for more than ten years, and had never liked him.[3] He had always thought George Custer overly proud and impulsive. The captain removed a piece of paper and the stub of a pencil from a pocket on his uniform, wrote George's name on it, and nailed it to the wooden stake marking the spot where the general had fallen.

"I went over the battlefield carefully with a view to determine how the fight was fought," a distressed Benteen wrote in a report two days after the conflict. "I arrived at the conclusion I have right now—that it was a rout, a panic, till the last man was killed. . . . George himself was responsible for the Little Big Horn action, and it is an injustice to attribute the blame to anyone else."[4] Benteen had been under George's command, ordered to reinforce his beleaguered troops at the Battle of the Little Bighorn. For reasons that would be debated by Benteen for the rest of his life, he did not come to George's aid.[5]

---

* A few opposing accounts of the aftermath of the battle report on the condition of Custer's remains, and claim that the body was untouched (i.e., Charles Hofling, *Custer and the Little Big Horn*). According to Chris Kortlander, director of the Custer Battlefield Museum, 260 men died at the Battle of the Little Bighorn, and 210 of those troops were with Custer at the Last Stand.

During the battle, Elizabeth Bacon Custer was only a few hundred miles away, in the Dakota Territory, waiting bravely for news of the expedition. The escalation of the Great Sioux War had brought the 7th Cavalry to the frontier, and where George went, Elizabeth followed.

One of the most charming and controversial soldiers the country ever produced, George Armstrong Custer and his equally delightful and charming bride were devoted to one another. They valued the time they spent together in the field and at their never-permanent homes at various army posts. Many times, Elizabeth lived in a tent alongside members of the 7th Cavalry.

Over the twelve years the Custers were together, Elizabeth had lived history. She and George had honeymooned in war zones during the waning years of the Civil War, and she had witnessed the surrender of Robert E. Lee at the Appomattox Court House. (She was later given the table at which the terms of surrender were signed.) Elizabeth embarked upon her frontier life following the Civil War, when George's regiment was sent to Texas to facilitate Reconstruction, and later, to the Great Plains states as an "Indian fighter." Her life was a series of thrilling adventures that lasted until the memorable day when Custer and his troops made their immortal last stand against the Sioux Indians.

During the times they were separated, George and Elizabeth wrote to each other constantly, and it was rumored that she was a collaborator on his memoirs. After Little Bighorn, Elizabeth relocated to New York City and wrote three wildly popular books about their adventures on the frontier, along with countless newspaper and magazine articles. She made it a point to correspond with the veterans who had campaigned with George, at times handwriting more than 300 such letters in a year. Every tie to her husband was sacred to her. She lectured all over the country, both to honor her husband and to refute any disparaging stories that may have arisen around the legend of "the Boy General." She wrote with pride of their time together, and spoke of the Native Americans without bitterness or resentment. She helped to shape history's view of General George Armstrong Custer, creating a larger-than-life image of the man, and of the Battle of the Little Bighorn on June 25, 1876. From that day forward, Elizabeth lived to glorify her husband's memory.

This book is the story behind the image she created—the story of a celebrity couple who had to deal with petty rumors, betrayals, and the real uncertainty and discomfort of army life. It's also the story of a couple very much in love, and how their vast adventures shaped the American West.

CHAPTER ONE

BEFORE GEORGE

A persistent woman sees what there is to be seen.

—ELIZABETH CUSTER, NOVEMBER 24, 1885

An exquisitely framed photograph of George Custer rested on an easel next to the lectern. Elizabeth Bacon Custer, George's devoted wife, studied her husband's image as she sat in the meeting hall at John Street Church in Lowell, Massachusetts, on January 31, 1894. Hundreds of flowers surrounded the enlarged picture—the last one taken of Custer, in late April 1876. Adorned in a blue uniform decorated with rows of brass buttons, medals, and intricately woven, golden shoulder braids, he was the model of strength and confidence. His short hair was neatly combed, and his thick mustache was smoothed down over his lips.[1]

The room was filled with ladies dressed in their finest Sunday clothes, sitting at numerous tables arrayed around the large hall. They were giddy with excitement and chatted briskly while sipping coffee and tea. Elizabeth's seat was at a long table for ten placed upon a dais. She was the guest of honor, flanked on either side by overly attentive women continuously thanking her for being with them.[2]

Elizabeth was an attractive, petite, fifty-one-year-old woman with a strong face and quiet, intelligent eyes. The black and gray taffeta dress she wore was unassuming but stylish. Her attention was drawn away from the photograph of her husband when a spry, elderly woman with light blue-gray eyes made her way to the podium.

As the woman welcomed guests to the lecture, several male members of the church filtered into the back of the room and stood respectfully, waiting for the program to begin. Elizabeth was introduced as the keynote speaker, and as she rose from her chair, radiant and poised, the entire room was galvanized into sudden and tumultuous applause. She stood in simple, dignified response to the ovation and smiled sweetly to her left, then to her right. After everyone had taken their seats, Elizabeth expressed her appreciation for the kind reception.

"My husband was killed more than seventeen years ago at the Battle of the Little Bighorn," she said in a crisp, cultured voice. "I believe he had many enemies there, and none of them were Indians. His rivals sent him on a suicide mission, with too few troops and ammunition."[3] After a few more opening remarks, Elizabeth went on to tell the enraptured audience about her life on the frontier. An article in the Lowell, Massachusetts, *Daily Sun* described the lecture as "entertaining and informal."

> *Mrs. Custer began with a description of the garrison of the far west, the palisades, construction, the officers' quarters, the stables, the general mess. She then spoke*

of life as an Army dependent and elaborated on the ladies who followed their soldier husbands to the frontier, their duties, amusements, etc. Her description of a typical social gathering around a none-too-elegant piano to sing songs of the day, the higher music and the religious melodies, [was] alternatively humorous and touching, and it delighted the audience. No less interesting [was] her description of the long hunts participated in by the officers and men. The frolicking of her husband's 40 hounds with their well groomed horses, the start of their hunts with their thermometer 20 and 30 degrees below zero, and their return with deer and other game . . .

The occasional gossiping women of garrison life received attention, and Mrs. Custer naively described the remedies. The husbands of such women received intimations of transfers to distant parts, and that was sufficient.

The lecture was entertaining throughout and was highly appreciated by all who attended.[4]

The captivated audience gave Elizabeth another round of applause at the conclusion of her talk. She smiled appreciatively and glanced at George's portrait before returning to her seat.[5] Since George's death, Elizabeth had devoted herself to safeguarding his reputation as a military leader and husband from men like Captain Frederick Benteen who resented his fame.[6]

Almost from the moment Elizabeth Bacon and George Custer first saw each other in 1862, they were smitten with one another. "How I watched her every motion . . . ," George wrote of his initial encounter with Elizabeth.[7] He once told her he would "give up every earthly hope to gain her love."[8]

Born on April 8, 1842, on the shores of Lake Erie in Monroe, Michigan, Elizabeth Clift Bacon, named after her paternal grandmother, was one of four children, including two sisters who died in infancy and a brother who died at the age of eight. Fearful of losing Elizabeth to illness or accident, Elizabeth Custer's father, Judge Daniel Bacon, and her mother, Eleanor Sophia Page (known as Sophia), were overly protective of her. At times Elizabeth rebelled against their rules and restrictions, which, for example, prohibited her from playing with other children. Whenever her parents were distracted, she snuck away to do as she pleased. Each time her frantic mother would find her and drag her home again.

Sophia subscribed to severe methods of punishment that included locking Elizabeth in a closet or forcing her to remain in bed. The harsh treatment had the desired effect. Driven to tears, Elizabeth would apologize for her actions and promise never to break the rules again.[9]

The tragic loss of Sophia's other three children had left her sad and withdrawn. Elizabeth tried to help her mother through her depression, but with little success.

The occasional song Elizabeth played on the piano Sophia had given her on her eleventh birthday pleased her, but the mood was short-lived. She seemed to only take special notice of Elizabeth when she memorized Scripture. Sophia insisted that Elizabeth study long passages from the Bible so she would learn about humility and modesty.[10] She also served as an example of Christian giving; with Elizabeth in tow, Sophia would visit the homes of indigent and sick families in the area, delivering food and clothing.[11]

In the summer of 1854, when Elizabeth was barely twelve years old, Sophia died of dysentery. On August 27, she recorded her thoughts about her mother's passing in the journal she had already kept for more than two years:

> *Mother is sleeping her last great sleep from which she will never wake up, no never . . . Two weeks ago my mother was laid in the cold ground and as I stood by that open grave and felt—oh! God only knows what anguish filled my heart. O! Why did they put my mother in that great black coffin and screw the lid down so tight?*[12]

Judge Bacon was devastated by his wife's death, and for a brief time left the family home in order to grieve alone. He sent Elizabeth to live with her aunt, feeling she would receive the comfort she needed from her mother's sister. Several months passed before the judge saw his daughter again, at which time he enrolled her in a primary school in Monroe, Michigan, the Young Ladies' Seminary and Collegiate Institute, more commonly known as Boyd's Seminary.

In the fall of 1858, Judge Bacon registered Elizabeth at a boarding school in Auburn, New York.

Elizabeth continued to grieve her mother's death, and dealt with the tragedy by concentrating on her studies. "No one knows how much I lost but myself," she wrote in her journal in the winter of 1858, about Sophia's passing. "Although sometimes I give up in despair and say I can't," she added, "when I think how sweet Mother used to love to have me diligent, I am inspired with new hope."[13]

Judge Bacon visited his daughter often at the school and was pleased with how well she was adjusting. In addition to the traditional subjects of literature, history, and mathematics (in which she excelled), Elizabeth took courses in gardening, art, music, and French. Her father was not only proud of her academic accomplishments, but also with how beautiful she had become. During her time away from home she had blossomed from a girl into a woman. At sixteen, Elizabeth attracted the attention of many young men; according to her journal, she was well aware of the effect she had on the opposite sex, and was not above using it to get what she wanted.[14]

Although she occasionally toyed with the affections of hopeful suitors, she was primarily interested in her schoolwork and in becoming an artist and a writer. She specifically wanted to work for a newspaper.[15] Married men made advances toward the teenaged Elizabeth, but she held her own against their unwanted gestures. She was not shy about vocalizing her disdain for such behavior, and on one occasion, she even slapped a doctor who tried to kiss her.

When Elizabeth wasn't preoccupied with her lessons, she dreamed of being in Monroe with her father. She wanted to take care of him and manage his household.[16] Any hope Elizabeth may have had that such a notion would become reality was dashed when the judge announced he had met and fallen in love with Rhoda Wells Pitts. Although Elizabeth was not initially pleased by the news, her attitude eventually softened. Rhoda was the forty-six-year-old widow of a successful New York businessman. She was financially solvent, and known for being congenial, as well as a good housekeeper and cook.

Judge Bacon and Rhoda were married in February 1859. When Elizabeth returned to Monroe from school later that year, she spent time getting to know her stepmother. Rhoda proved herself to be a truly caring and considerate person— so much so that Elizabeth soon came to call her "Mother." When Elizabeth became ill, Rhoda nursed her back to health. In several letters to her cousin, Rebecca Richmond, Elizabeth praised Rhoda's kindness and generosity. She recalled the time spent with her stepmother and father with great fondness: "How I miss my pleasant home!" she wrote to Rebecca in 1859. "Those Sunday suppers with fire blazing . . . those juicy steaks, smoking muffins, all the delicacies my mother knows so well to prepare. . . ."[17]

After more than a year's absence from school, Elizabeth returned to her studies. She graduated in 1862 as valedictorian of her class. She accepted her diploma wearing a beautiful dress Rhoda had made for her. According to Rebecca Richmond, who attended the ceremony, the dress was "white Swiss muslin, high in the neck, and closed at the waist." Rebecca later wrote to her parents, saying, "We were all proud of Elizabeth. When it came to her valedictory there was scarcely a dry eye, so many were there who had watched her through her motherless girlhood. Her father, who sat on the platform, was greatly affected."[18]

By the time Elizabeth graduated from Boyd's Seminary, more than two thousand of the men of Monroe County (roughly 10 percent of the population at that time) had joined the Union Army and gone to fight the rebellious Southern states. Judge Bacon read the newspaper aloud each evening at dinner, keeping his family abreast of the wartime happenings and the comings and goings of area volunteers. Soldiers passed by the Bacons' place en route to their homes or to various posts. Some were wounded and missing limbs and had to be helped along their way.

Elizabeth and her friends watched members of the 15th Michigan Regiment parade along the street and reverently waved them on. As they marched by, her dream of writing for a newspaper went with them, leaving in its place a new heart's desire—marrying a soldier.[19]

In spite of the decreased male population in Monroe during the war, Elizabeth never lacked for male attention. The few eligible bachelors who remained in town, including attorneys, businessmen, and church pastors, called on her after receiving her father's approval. She was flattered by the many admirers, but none of them held her interest.

In late 1862, Elizabeth and a few of her friends from school celebrated the Thanksgiving holiday by attending a party at their alma mater. Many soldiers, home on leave, were present at the seminary function, and sought out the company of Monroe's prettiest belles. Among the volunteers present at the party was George Armstrong Custer.

George lived with his sister and brother-in-law on the same street as the Bacons in Monroe, and although he and Elizabeth had seen one another around the neighborhood, they had never been formally introduced. By Thanksgiving of 1862, however, George's military reputation preceded him. A West Point graduate, he had made a name for himself serving under Major General George Brinton McClellan, rising quickly to the rank of lieutenant and fighting bravely at the First Battle of Bull Run.

When they met at Boyd's Seminary, Elizabeth offered her hand and George gently took it in his and smiled politely. They watched one another carefully while dancing in a quadrille opposite each other. When the music stopped, the two engaged in a brief conversation.[20]

"I believe your promotion has been very rapid," Elizabeth stated.

"I have been very fortunate," he answered humbly. They chatted for a few moments more before each going their separate ways.[21]

According to George's recollection of the meeting years later, he was "quite taken with dark-eyed Elizabeth, dressed in white with a red rose pinned in her hair."

"My heart could have told her of a promotion far more rapid in her power only to bestow. How I watched her every motion, and when she left . . . in that throng of youth and beauty she had reigned supreme."[22]

Elizabeth was not as taken with George as he was with her. She considered his hair (he had nearly shoulder-length, reddish-blond hair, and fierce blue eyes) and manner of dress pretentious. In a journal entry written on November 28, 1862, Elizabeth noted that "with the critical and hard eye of a girl, I decided I would never like him."[23]

For that brief moment in time, Elizabeth's opinion of George was akin to that of many of his peers. Men like Captain Frederick Benteen found him to be "arrogant, rash, with a will to succeed no matter the cost."[24]

CHAPTER TWO

Courting Elizabeth

Oh, Wifey, Wifey! One of those mustached, gift-striped and buttoned critters will get our Libbie yet.

—Judge Daniel Bacon to his wife, Rhoda, about the many young soldiers calling on their daughter, Elizabeth

A full moon hovered over South Monroe Street, and beams of light from the gigantic orb filtered though a cluster of clouds. Twenty-one-year-old George Armstrong Custer stumbled through the scene, helped along by a friend who steadied his walk and kept him from falling. Both men were dressed in the uniform of the 5th Cavalry, and both had been drinking. In fact, George was drunk. It was late, and apart from the two inebriated soldiers, the street was deserted.

It was the fall of 1861, and numerous leaves had dropped off the massive trees lining the thoroughfare, drifting across the path the men followed. George was making his way to his sister Ann Reed's home, where he had been staying while recovering from a slight illness contracted after the Battle of Bull Run.[1] George had carried dispatches to the Union troops holding their position against the Confederate

Army, lined up along Bull Run Creek near a railroad center called Manassas Junction in Virginia.[2] The battle had ended when the Union Army was ordered to fall back toward Washington, and the accompanying downpour of rain had left George suffering with chills and fever.[3] He was sent back to Monroe to recuperate, and as George's condition improved, he started venturing out to local taverns where his friends gathered.

Arm in arm with his school chum, an intoxicated George and his buddy staggered down the roadway, singing at the top of their lungs. The commotion woke his sister, who raced to the front window of her house, followed closely by her husband and children, to see who was disturbing the quiet, respectable neighborhood. George weaved back and forth over the cobblestone street, laughing at his obvious lack of balance.

Judge Bacon, who had been standing on his porch, smoking his pipe, noticed the pair of soldiers making their way toward the Reeds' home. He recognized George Custer's tall, lanky frame and watched him as he waved good-bye to the friend who had escorted him safely home. Disgusted by the soldier's behavior, the judge marched back into his own house and closed the door hard behind him.[4]

George was unaware that Judge Bacon had witnessed the scene. He also had no idea that Elizabeth Bacon had been gazing out of her upstairs bedroom window at the same moment. She wasn't surprised at the sight, having seen other young men who'd had too much to drink. She considered his actions standard fare, and the following morning, barely remembered the spectacle George had made of himself the night before.[5]

Elizabeth was preoccupied with thoughts of her unknown future and spent long hours in conversation with her cousin, Rebecca Richmond, discussing marriage and life thereafter. Elizabeth had many callers and admirers. One young man, a childhood sweetheart named Elliot Bates, wanted to take her for his bride. She, however, did not return his feelings.[6] Convinced she might never find someone with whom she would fall in love, Elizabeth noted in her journal that she would be forced to become a spinster. The idea was not pleasant to her. "To be one [a spinster] from necessity and one from pleasure are two different things," she wrote.[7]

Elizabeth's father and stepmother were concerned about the possibility of their daughter ending up alone, but that fear paled in comparison to their concern that George Custer could be the one to rescue her from such a fate. In general, they didn't want Elizabeth to marry a soldier because they worried he might be killed in battle, leaving their daughter a penniless widow. Specifically, the Bacons didn't want Elizabeth to marry George because it was rumored he was proficient at swearing, gambling, and frequenting saloons. They believed George was much too worldly for their prim, proper, and somewhat sheltered daughter.

After meeting Elizabeth on Thanksgiving Day in 1862 at Boyd's Seminary, George had set his sights on the intelligent beauty. He was not ignorant of her father's high standards for her suitors, nor was he a man to back down from a challenge. After learning that Judge Bacon had seen him the night he came home drunk in October 1861, he couldn't bring himself to do much more at first than stare admiringly at Elizabeth from across the church they attended together. She was intrigued by the attention.[8]

By the time George gathered up the nerve to ask Elizabeth's permission to call on her in mid-December 1862, she had learned all about the handsome army officer from a mutual acquaintance. George Armstrong Custer was born in New Rumley, Ohio, on December 5, 1839. His father, Emmanuel Custer, was a blacksmith, farmer, and justice of the peace in the small Midwestern town. His mother, Maria Ward Kirkpatrick, was a homemaker. Each had three children from earlier marriages, and the pair had five more children together, including George Armstrong, named after the Methodist minister in hopes that the first son from their union would become a member of the clergy. George was particularly close to his younger brothers, Nevin, Thomas, and Boston, and his half sister, Ann, who was fourteen years his senior.[9]

In 1851, shortly after Ann married David Reed, a businessman from Michigan, George went to live with them in Monroe. Emanuel and Maria Custer were overwhelmed with the number of children they had to raise and believed George would benefit from the opportunity. Indeed, George excelled in school, first attending the McNeely Normal School at Hopedale, Ohio, and then the Stebbins Academy in Monroe.[10]

After completing his studies at the academy, George accepted the responsibility of helping to support his parents and siblings, many of whom were struggling financially. From 1854 to 1856, George taught primary school, earning $26 a month for his efforts.[11] He liked making money, and believed the only way he could be in a position to earn more was to have an education. Although he believed in God and the Golden Rule, he did not feel called to become a member of the clergy. He wanted a military career.

George's desire to go to West Point was realized in May 1857 when Ohio representative John A. Bingham recommended him for an appointment. George was seventeen when he entered the four-year military academy, where he struggled with what he believed to be overly strict rules, as well as hazing from upperclassmen.[12] He received numerous demerits for the length of his yellow hair, his untidy room, his careless dress, for playing pranks on other students, and for gambling and fighting. He frequently participated in heated debates with students from Southern states who favored slavery. A staunch abolitionist, George and his other classmates from the North insisted that slavery should not be allowed and that a war over the issue was bound to occur.[13]

Letters from his family and young eligible women, enamored with George's looks and potential for becoming a high-ranking officer, kept him distracted from his studies and talk of war. Using a candle to see the paper and ink, he answered their correspondence late in the evening after his instructors had ordered lights out.

By the time George graduated from West Point in 1861, the fateful firing on Fort Sumter had brought the country into the long-anticipated Civil War. George was commissioned with the rank of second lieutenant and ordered to report for duty in Washington, D.C. After making a brief stop in New York to purchase his officer's uniform, consisting of saber, revolver, sash, and spurs, he arrived at his post, eager to serve with the 2nd Cavalry. From Washington he was ordered to travel under cover of darkness to Centerville, Virginia, to deliver special messages to General Irvin McDowell.

Shortly after he arrived in Centerville, he was informed that he would be helping in the fight against the Confederates at Bull Run Creek, near the Manassas railway station. His particular job was to help protect a regiment that was preparing cannons for battle. A surprise attack by the Rebels from the rear scattered the Union Army and forced them to retreat. George held his position with the members of the platoon he commanded and waited for orders to regroup, but, outnumbered and outmaneuvered, the commanders for the North agreed to return to the capital to assess the damage and casualties, and to plan another charge at a later date.[14]

As George was one of the few officers who did not break ranks and run during the fight at Bull Run, official reports made mention that he was a "cool-headed youngster under fire."[15] A downpour of rain soaked the Union troops as they headed back to Washington; for hours, they slogged through mud and blowing debris. By the time many of them reached the Potomac, they were sick with colds and the flu. George was among those who became ill and was sent to his sister's home in Monroe to get well. This is when the lovely Miss Bacon first caught his eye. As soon as George's health improved, he was ordered to join the other men in his company in Washington. When he arrived he learned that there was to be another attack on Manassas and that the 2nd Cavalry had been redesignated the 5th Cavalry, under a program designed to enlarge the cavalry corps.

In February 1862, General George McClellan ordered the Union Army to advance into Virginia. George got a chance to lead a charge against a Confederate picket line holding a hill above the battlefield. George called the troops to attention and ordered them to follow him. Spurring his horse, he dashed up the hill in a headlong gallop. He did not look back, but he could hear the men following closely behind him. The Confederates held their ground, but only for a moment. The onrushing cavalry, led by the wild-whooping and saber-swinging George, proved to be too much for them, and the Rebels fled the scene. With the enemy routed, the 5th Cavalry took possession of the hilltop.[16]

After leading his men into the first major fight with the Southern forces, George took on the duty of observation officer at the Second Battle of Bull Run. The observations were conducted from a giant, gas-filled balloon. His nighttime ascensions proved most helpful in determining the strength and position of the opposing army. On the ground George accompanied General McClellan and Union troops in pursuit of the Confederates. He managed to locate the Rebels on the banks of the Chickahominy River. There was no bridge, so George found a spot in the river that was shallow enough for his regiment to wade across to the other side. His sharp thinking and daring earned him two citations and a promotion to captain.[17]

When he returned to Monroe in November 1862, news of his accomplishments had reached his extremely proud family, who happily greeted him. George's war-hero status made little impression on Judge Bacon, however. He had no intention of allowing his only child to become involved with a military man, "who had no money but his pay." Judge Bacon also did not want Elizabeth to be tied to a soldier who might become disabled. "I do not want you to be burdened with the responsibility of caring for another to that extent," he told her.[18]

Despite the judge's warning, Elizabeth grew fond of George. Over time, his charm and his relentless pursuit overcame her first impressions. George kept vigil outside her home, waiting for a chance to speak with her every time she left the house. He accompanied Elizabeth as she ran various errands and during visits to friends and neighbors.

In April 1863, Judge Bacon and George began corresponding when Judge Bacon asked George to provide him with accounts from the front line of battle. Although the two men became friends through the letters they exchanged, Judge Bacon remained convinced his daughter should not marry a soldier.

In May 1863, George pleaded with Elizabeth to marry him. She turned him down, and later regretted not accepting his proposal. "I cannot tell anyone how badly I feel," she noted in her journal. "No one can ever know, but I will write some of the deep and tender feelings I cannot suppress. . . . I cannot but mourn to think I have a saddened life. . . . He is noble, brave, and generous, and he loves, I believe, with an intensity that few know of or as few ever can love."[19]

Unwilling to give up on the thought of a life with Elizabeth, George employed a tactic he hoped would provoke a response. On September 28, 1863, he attended a party he knew Elizabeth would not miss. When she arrived, George made sure she saw him flirting with another girl. The performance had the desired effect. Elizabeth and George met in the parlor of the home where the party was being held, and the two sat together and talked. He entreated Elizabeth to say she would never leave him.[20]

Judge Bacon was annoyed when he was told of George's attentions to Elizabeth. He forbade his daughter from having any more to do with the decorated soldier. The thought of being denied George's company upset her more than she had anticipated. Elizabeth confessed in her journal that she was fonder of him than she realized. "He is so bright I couldn't help but like him," she wrote. Elizabeth sent George a note to let him know her father disapproved of them spending time together. Elizabeth also wrote a note to her father, apologizing for risking a "crisis in their relationship."

"I did it all for you," she wrote to Judge Bacon. "I like him [George] very well, and it is pleasant always to have an escort to depend on. But I am sorry I have been with him so much, and you will never see me in the street with him again, and never at the house except to say good-bye. I told him never to meet me, and he has the sense to understand. But I did not promise never to see him again. But I will not cause you any more trouble, be sure."[21]

George knew he could never persuade Elizabeth to go against her father's wishes, but he was confident that in time, the judge would change his mind about him. The two men were able to discuss the matter briefly in September 1863. During the polite conversation, George informed Judge Bacon that he would be leaving for Virginia.

Elizabeth was sad when her father broke the news of George's departure, confiding in her journal:

I felt so sorry for him. I think I had something to do with his going. I believe he liked me and felt my refusal to go with him. I wish him success . . . 'Tis best as it is, for I never should encourage such attentions when I know that I cannot return them with the right spirit. Good-bye to him then! I shall miss his daily walk up and down the street, for he walks and rides superbly. He was in too much haste, tho' I admired his perseverance.[22]

Elizabeth wasn't the only one who admired George's perseverance. The 5th Michigan Cavalry did as well. His much-talked-about, steadfast qualities prompted other able-bodied recruits to join the Union Army. Cavalry soldiers wanted to serve alongside the "daring young boy with the golden locks" who had risen to the rank of captain in such a short period of time.[23]

George had proven himself to be an exceptional soldier on many occasions in 1863. In June of that year, George and the other cavalry members were on a scouting mission near the Blue Ridge Mountains. Suddenly, a force of Confederate cavalry overtook them. The 5th Michigan Cavalry was putting up a valiant fight when additional Rebel soldiers, led by Jeb Stuart, arrived on the scene. Saber clanged against saber as men shouted wildly and horses reared. Pistols cracked, and dust and smoke rose up in clouds. Through the noise and the gun smoke came a shout like a bugle call: "Come on, boys! Come on!" It was George, swinging his saber and riding straight toward Stuart's men. The men spurred forward to follow the yellow hair that shone through the dust like a bright flag.

The fighting was eventually reduced to hand-to-hand combat. Custer and his 5th Cavalry troops were triumphant, capturing one hundred prisoners and a Rebel banner. At the age of twenty-three, in June 1863, he was promoted to brevat, or temporary, brigadier general, U.S. Volunteers.[24]

News of his promotion was well publicized. Some applauded George's advancement, but others, including fellow soldier Frederick Benteen, resented him for it. Benteen, who was patrolling the Saline River in Arkansas at the time George was fighting with Southern troops, was annoyed by the report. He had yet to formally meet George Custer, but the ambitious cavalryman's reputation was pervasive. Years later, Benteen expressed his displeasure to the commander of the Cavalry Corps of the Army of the Potomac, Major General Philip Sheridan. "The best I could do is colonel," he complained when the major general asked about his Civil War career. "I had no political influence to forward me in rank or assist me in any way whatsoever."[25]

George wrote to Judge Bacon about his success on the battlefield, the particulars about the change in command, and the reorganization of the Army of the Potomac. He also included kind wishes for Judge Bacon's wife and daughter. George hoped that Elizabeth would also read the letters. Eventually, George dared to ask the judge if he might correspond with Elizabeth, though the two had already been secretly exchanging messages through letters to a mutual friend. Judge Bacon gave in to George's request, noting in a letter to the officer that he believed in his sincerity. "I have always admired you, and am now more than gratified at your well-earned reputation and high and exalted position. The evening you left here I had a full and free interview with Libbie and shall talk with her more upon this important subject which she is at full liberty to communicate with you." Shortly after receiving permission to write to one another, Elizabeth penned the first of hundreds of letters to George.[26]

Elizabeth also recorded her thoughts about the man she called her "beloved star" in her journal. "Love him! I have loved him all the time, and I need no clearer index of past feelings than this old book," she wrote. "I have written once of his taking my hand and kissing it and how he looked and how I felt. O' tho he kissed me when he was here last, my lips used to the thrill after I had left him and was in bed. Affectionate, I never saw a man more so."[27]

From October 1863 to February 1864, the pair courted strictly through the mail, as George was sent first to Rappahannock in eastern Virginia, and then on to Bristoe Station and Buckland Mills, where the 5th Michigan Cavalry was engaged in fierce battles. George wasn't able to write to Elizabeth as often as he would have liked, but she understood and filled in the gaps with additional correspondence to him. Although all of her letters spoke of her devotion to him and their future together, some expressed concern for George's well-being, and apprehension about getting married too quickly.[28] In December 1863, she wrote:

> You are coming, are you not, for the holidays? If so, I might relent. . . . Father accuses me of trifling, says, "You must not keep Armstrong waiting." But neither you nor he can know what preparations are needed for such an Event, an Event it takes at least a year to prepare for. After I am a soldier's wife, I will not urge you to leave your duty oftener than I can help. . . . Oh, what better argument can I offer than that I long to see you? The worst about loving a soldier is that he is as likely to die as to live . . . and how should I feel if my soldier should die before I have gratified his heart's desire?[29]

George was forthcoming in his letters about his feelings for Elizabeth, as well as his own vices. He confessed to her his "delight in playing cards and attending horse races," adding: "Scarcely a pleasant day passes that the officers of this division do not assemble to witness and stake money on races between favorite horses. Even General Pleasanton sometimes lends his presence, and General Kilpatrick invariably does. Between the latter and myself, frequent wagers have been laid."[30] Not only did George admit to his affinity for games of chance, but also for cursing. "I seldom indulge in it," he explained, "except when I am angry, and then it seems to afford me so much satisfaction . . ."[31]

Nonetheless, George was eager to make Elizabeth his wife and asked that they be married in early February 1864. Although she was nervous about leaving home and assuming the responsibility of being Mrs. Custer, she finally agreed.

While George was leading his regiment into battle against the Confederate Army marching toward Pennsylvania, Elizabeth was planning their wedding. She wrote to her cousin Rebecca about the upcoming nuptials and the material she wanted to use to make her gown. As Elizabeth anticipated questions about George's character, she noted the qualities she most admired in him—stretching the truth a bit in the process. "I do not say Armstrong is without faults. But he never tastes liquor, nor frequents the gaming-table, and though not a professing Christian, yet respects religion."[32]

George Custer and Elizabeth Bacon were married on February 9, 1864, at six o'clock in the evening at Monroe's Presbyterian church. The bride wore a white dress made of silk material from New York. Her veil floated back from a bunch of orange blossoms fixed above the brow. Her trousseau consisted of a large variety of dresses and included "a waterproof cape with arm-holes, buttoned from head to foot," and an "opera cloak with merino, silk-lined, that included a silk hood."[33]

George wore his full-dress uniform to the wedding, and many family members and friends were there, including George's brother Tom, whom he hadn't seen in more than four years. More than three hundred people were in attendance to celebrate the nuptials, followed by a reception at the Bacon home. Judge Bacon and his wife gave their daughter a Bible for a wedding present. To George, they gave their dearest possession—Elizabeth.[34]

CHAPTER THREE

NEWLYWEDS

General Custer has elements of character which will develop . . . and, dear girl, some of that development rests with you.

—ELIZABETH CUSTER'S FRIEND, LAURA NOBLE, ABOUT HER RELATIONSHIP WITH GEORGE, JANUARY 1864

Elizabeth paraded proudly around a small table set with a pristinely polished silver tea service and silver dinnerware. The elegant tea service came from the men in George's command, the 7th Michigan Cavalry. The dinnerware was a gift from the 1st Vermont Cavalry. Both were not only generous wedding presents, but also a show of support for the Boy General and his leadership skills.

Elizabeth adjusted a large, ceramic vase in the center of the table and stood back to admire the scene. Hanging over the table was a large photograph of George, resplendent in his crisp uniform. Elizabeth smiled at the image staring back at her. Eliza Brown, the Custers' capable cook and maid, watched the delighted bride through a crack in the kitchen door as she continued to fuss with the items on the table in an effort to make everything as perfect as possible.[1]

A myriad of troops was hustling around outside the sturdy two-story farmhouse in Culpeper County, Virginia, near the small town of Stevensburg, where Elizabeth and her new husband made their home. George rode into the winter encampment of the Union Army, barking orders at his regiment to get to their bunks and prepare for the evening meal. Hundreds of soldiers rushed about, doing their duties as ordered. Many of the men who made up the crude post were young and eager, while others were much more senior, with gray hair and weathered faces. From her position on the porch, Elizabeth noted George's imposing figure among his troops; his uniform hung well on his tall frame, with his saber and scabbard strapped to his waist and held in place with a silk sash.[2]

Before swinging easily out of his saddle, George scanned the area beyond the prairie road leading to the campsite. In the near distance he could see numerous furrows of glistening jet-black sod and a lone farmer guiding a plow pulled by a mule team. Smoke from a nearby chimney lifted lazy blue wreaths into the sky. George called out to one of his older officers and issued instructions Elizabeth could barely hear. She glided over to George's side just as the soldier left to carry out his job.

"Do they obey you?" she asked. "Yes," George replied, laughing, "and I shall reduce you to subjection sometime."[3] Elizabeth laughed out loud at the notion. She slid her arm into the crook of his elbow as they walked slowly toward their quarters. The soldiers under George were polite and eager, saluting him as he passed.

"It's fortunate such manners aren't expected from your family," Elizabeth teased.

"You could be punished for insubordination," he said, laughing along with her. "Camp followers have rules to adhere to as well as the troops," George added. The pair strode off in the direction of their home.

The Custers were distracted by a half-dozen Conestoga wagons being escorted into camp by a group of soldiers.[4] George excused himself and left his wife to speak to one of the men with the party as he dismounted his horse. They exchanged salutes and began a conversation that Elizabeth couldn't hear. While waiting for her husband to rejoin her, three women passengers stepped out of the wagon carrying parcels. They were striking women, all with blue eyes and an abundance of red-brown hair, the tint of which turned the heads of most of the soldiers around. Elizabeth watched curiously as the ladies were led away by courteous enlisted men. Eliza stepped outside as they passed by.

"Camp followers," she explained to an inquisitive Elizabeth. "They call themselves laundresses, but that's not exactly so."[5]

Few women with Elizabeth's background ever accompanied their husbands to primitive posts; most of the women who dared travel with the troops were servants or prostitutes. Even in her sheltered home, Elizabeth had heard rumors about such women—and one of them involved George and a "camp follower" named Annie Elinor James.[6] According to Annie herself, she "went to the front as the friend and companion of General Custer" in the summer of 1863. Since that time she had been arrested by the Union government and charged with being a Confederate spy. Although Annie denied being a spy, she did admit that she had depended on the kindness of Union officers for her care, saying, "I have been the guest of different officers; they furnished me with horses, orderlies, escorts, sentinels at my tent or quarters, rations, etc." The War Department believed there was more to it than that and was holding her at the Old Capitol Prison until a hearing could be conducted. [7]

One of the new camp followers caught George's eye as she passed by him. They exchanged smiles and he politely nodded to her. For a brief moment Elizabeth considered those rumors about the relationship between George and Annie, and wondered if they might not have been too far from the truth. Her countenance fell a bit, and she tried not to let it show as George turned to face her. He took Elizabeth's hand in his, kissed it gently, and then led her to their quarters, closing the door behind them. [8]

The Custers had been on the move since the moment they had taken their vows. During their eight-day honeymoon to New York, which included stops in between to visit family members, the newlyweds went to West Point. While George spoke with favorite teachers and former classmates, some of the cadets—enamored with Elizabeth's beauty and charm—kept her company. Once the pair were on their way again, George expressed his disapproval over the attention she had received from the other men. On February 15, 1864, she wrote to her father about her new husband's jealous reaction. "On the train going back I was amazed to see my blithe bridegroom turned into an incarnated thundercloud," Elizabeth recalled years later in her memoirs. "'But,' I tearfully protested, '. . . the cadets who showed me lovers' walk were like school-boys with their shy ways and nice, clean, friendly faces. . . .' Oh, I quite expected to be sent home to my parents, till I took courage to say, 'Well, you left me with them, Autie!' "[9] (Autie was Elizabeth's pet name for George. The nickname was initially given to him by his family when he was four years old because he had a hard time pronouncing his middle name.)

George regretted his actions and apologized to Elizabeth for his outburst. They enjoyed their time together until the telegrams ordering George to Washington increased in number and urgency. Their time at the capital was brief, but no less memorable for its duration. Elizabeth made the acquaintance of several distinguished military leaders, including Brigadier General Alexander Webb, chief of artillery of the Army of the Potomac, and General Ulysses S. Grant.

From Washington, the Custers left for Virginia and the rugged outpost that would serve as Elizabeth's introduction to life as an army wife. She was impressed with the attention George garnered everywhere they went. "None of the other generals receive half the attention, and their arrivals are scarcely noticed in the papers," she informed her parents. "I am so amazed at his reputation . . . I wonder his head is not turned. Tho not disposed to put on airs, I find it very agreeable to be the wife of a man so generally known and respected."[10]

George made every effort to shower his bride with niceties that would make her stay at the outpost more comfortable. When they arrived at Stevensburg, he gave her a pony and taught her how to ride like an experienced cavalryman. She practiced alongside columns of troops on horseback, bringing up the rear with the supply wagons. She later noted in her journal that whenever she would glance over at her husband, he was proudly watching her. "He had only the utmost patience," she observed, "and [I] heard constant commendations if I got the pony into his clumpety little canter."[11]

By late March 1864, George was on his way to Richmond with his Michigan Brigade. Elizabeth went back to Washington to wait for her husband's safe return from battle. She wrote in her journal, "Washington was a bewildering and delightful place." The corridors of the hotels were "filled with the officers on leave in shining new uniforms, and the city was made gay from having so many troops."[12]

The city offered numerous distractions, but Elizabeth's thoughts remained with George. News of his victories regularly made the newspapers. Holed up in her room at a boardinghouse on Sixth Street, Elizabeth pored over George's correspondence and the articles about his bravery in various publications. A March 19, 1864, edition of *Harper's Weekly* featured a drawing of George leading a charge on horseback, brandishing his sword. Reading through the account of his heroic efforts in Charlottesville, where George had helped to destroy Confederate supplies, made her miss him desperately. "I will not attempt to tell you how lonely I am," she informed her parents in a letter written in April 1864. "It was a far worse trial than I anticipated to part from my husband. And yet I am prouder far to be his wife than I would be to be Mrs. Lincoln or a queen."[13]

Elizabeth was not ignorant of the fact that George's continued success on the battlefront would further his army career. She attempted to aid him in his efforts by spending time with political and military leaders who frequented the capital. Michigan representative F. W. Kellogg and his wife, Almira, some of George's key supporters, squired Elizabeth around town, making sure to introduce her to influential figures. One of the most important was President Abraham Lincoln. Elizabeth was nervous and content simply to shake his hand and continue on her way, but the president had other ideas. She wrote to her parents about their meeting: "At the mention of my name, he took my hand again very cordially and said, 'So this is the young woman whose husband goes into a charge with a whoop and a shout. . . .' I am quite a Lincoln girl now."[14]

Between Elizabeth's charm and George's more-than-capable soldiering, Custer came to be thought of as indispensable to the Union Army. Major General Philip Sheridan, leader of the Cavalry Corps of the Army of the Potomac, called George one of his "dependables."[15]

George and Elizabeth consistently wrote to one another. She shared news from Washington with him, and he kept her abreast of what was happening with his command. "We had a splendid review today," he noted in his correspondence, dated April 23, 1864. "General Sheridan reviewed the entire Division. My Brigade never looked better. I was more than proud of it. We compared favorably with other Brigades. I wished my little girl might have been present to enjoy the sight. . . . When I think of the sacrifices you have made for me, the troubles and trials you have endured to make me happy, the debt of gratitude you have placed me under, my heart almost fails me to think I have only the devotion of my life to offer you in return."[16]

While the newlyweds explored the capital and enjoyed George's rising reputation with the army, the battle-worn members of the 10th Missouri Cavalry tended to their wounded and dying in a makeshift camp along the banks of the crooked Red River in Northwest Louisiana. A few days had passed since their attack on the town of Pleasant Hill. Captain Frederick Benteen had been part of the raid, leading his regiment into the Confederate-controlled area in early April 1864. The scene was one of the bloodiest assaults of the Civil War west of the Mississippi River.

Benteen sat on a supply crate inside his tent, reviewing his handwritten account of the incident. A light rain tapped on the canvas overhead, and the sound of distant rolling thunder pried him from his seat. He pulled back the flap to inspect the dreary weather and was immediately met by an enlisted man with the daily dispatches. The gruff officer returned the soldier's salute, took the paperwork from him, and pulled the flap of the tent back down.[17]

The Virginia-born commander was exhausted, short on words, and short on patience. According to the men who served under him, he was gruff and generally irritable. They were familiar with his surly disposition and did not like to disturb him unless it was absolutely necessary. In spite of his often-cantankerous mood, his troops respected his leadership ability and his fierce loyalty to the North. In 1862, Benteen had had his own father, Theodore Charles Benteen, arrested for blockade-running. He had little appreciation for wartime celebrities like George Custer or George Pickett, a popular and dapper West Point cadet and Confederate Army officer.[18]

In addition to examining the war dispatches, Benteen also read newspaper and magazine articles that were sometimes included in the communications about the war's progress. Benteen's response to seeing Custer's image on the cover of *Harper's Weekly* was substantially different from Elizabeth's. He thought that Custer, however effective his military maneuvers were, was self-serving, brash, and irresponsible. The reports that Elizabeth was being presented to Washington's elite did not sit well with him, either. Benteen felt Elizabeth was pompous, condescending, and undeserving of the attention she received. In letters he wrote to his wife, Catherine, years after the Civil War had ended, he noted that Elizabeth was "as cold-blooded a woman as I ever knew, in which respect the pair [George and Elizabeth] were admirably mated."[19]

The popular Mrs. Custer missed her parents and Monroe but did not feel badly about leaving them behind for her new life as a celebrated officer's wife. In the spring of 1864, George was granted a short time away from his post, and he hurried to Washington to be with his bride. "At times I am so homesick," she wrote to her mother in May 1864, "but I do not regret the exchange. . . . Oh, what a surprise! Generals Sheridan and Torbet wanted something done in Washington and gave Autie 48 hours here in which to accomplish it. I was talking to a lady who was calling on me about Autie when the door burst open. He rushed upstairs so fast the people thought the house was on fire. . . . How happy I am with Autie and our life here."[20]

George returned from his assignment at the capital and his brief visit with his wife just in time to learn he was being passed over for promotion to commander of the cavalry's entire 3rd Division. General Ulysses S. Grant, as head of the Army of the Potomac, wanted his closest military friends in charge of important areas. Although George was not among this group, General Sheridan— one of Grant's most trusted advisors—entreated Grant to make good use of Custer's leadership abilities. At Gettysburg, Custer had led the Union cavalry through a series of headlong charges against Jeb Stuart and the Confederate Army. General Sheridan wanted to reward his efforts by giving him command of a cavalry division. He even recommended that George be promoted to the rank of major general.[21]

On May 14, 1864, George wrote Elizabeth a letter from Rexall's Landing on the river in Virginia with news of his promotion to captain of the 5th Cavalry. At the time of promotion, George was still a brevet major general. General Sheridan was successful in persuading General Grant to give George a permanent ranking. His military career continued to be on the rise, earning him a certain level of notoriety, and Elizabeth, many social opportunities. It came with a price, however; Elizabeth missed George terribly and she feared for his safety.

George wrote to Elizabeth about his battle experiences near Cold Harbor, Virginia:

> *We have passed through days of carnage, and have lost heavily. . . . The Michigan Brigade has covered itself with undying glory. We destroyed railroads, and commands in Lee's rear, which was mentioned in Sheridan's report to General Grant. . . . I led a charge in which we mortally wounded General Stuart and captured a battery of three cannons and a large number of prisoners. General Sheridan sent an aide on the battlefield with his congratulations. So did General Merritt. The Michigan Brigade is at the top of the ladder. . . . I enclose some honeysuckle I plucked.*[22]

When Elizabeth wasn't writing long letters to George and sharing news of the influential characters she met while visiting the Capitol, she was devouring any story about him that made the papers. His heroic struggles on June 9, 1864, at Cold Harbor in Central Virginia were the front-page story of the *Monroe Monitor*, which Judge Bacon sent to Elizabeth from her hometown. Cold Harbor was one of the bloodiest battles in America's history. Thousands of Union soldiers were killed or wounded in a frontal assault against the fortified troops of Confederate general Robert E. Lee. Heavy losses were sustained. Several of the men in George's division were gunned down and died from their wounds, and George himself was shot while pulling a wounded soldier to safety.[23]

The June 15 edition of the *Monroe Monitor* reported that "George Custer, prior to being struck on the shoulder and arm by a spent ammunition, had rescued the brigade's flag and color bearer who had been shot and mortally wounded. Not wanting to leave the young color bearer on the field to be shot again, Custer carried the man out of harm's way."[24] A *New York Tribune* article from August 1864 reported that George Custer was a "first-class hero":

> *Stories of his daring will be told around many a hearth-stone after the [brigade's] old flag again kisses the breeze. . . . No officer in the ranks of the Union Army entertains for the rebel enemy more contempt than General Custer, and probably no cavalry officer in our army is better known or more feared than he. Always circumspect, never rash, and viewing the circumstances of the ground at a glance, and like the eagle watching*

his prey from some mountain crag, sweeps down upon his adversary and seldom fails in achieving a signal success. Frank and independent in demeanor, General Custer unites the qualities of a true gentleman with that of the accomplished and fearless soldier. [25]

Although Elizabeth was proud of George's conduct and gallantry, she was rattled by how close he had come to death. She idolized her husband, and was captivated by his devotion and heroics, along with other women who read the accounts of his deeds. When Elizabeth finally received a letter from George saying that he was safe and well, she was elated. "Oh, my darling," she responded, "what have I not endured in torture for the past fortnight. I will learn to be brave, but you know, dear, I can't learn all at once. Father and Mother write me I am not alone in anxiety—they bear it with me." [26] Although she had her parents' empathy, they were miles away in Monroe, Michigan, and Elizabeth, living in Washington, D.C., had to endure the fretful separation from George alone.

George was acutely aware of the risks involved with being a soldier during wartime, and he did not want Elizabeth to endure financial hardship if something dire should happen. He put her in charge of their finances and entrusted her with a sizable portion of his monthly income. Custer earned $290 a month, of which he kept $100 for his living expenses, sending the balance to Elizabeth. [27] George encouraged her to manage the money well so that she would have funds to support herself if he were killed in battle. Elizabeth was ignorant about money matters at first; her father had always taken care of family finances. She quickly learned the importance of spending wisely, however. She believed that not only should she be a good steward in case of emergency, but also that she should save for the child she hoped she and George would have sooner rather than later.[28]

Rather than splurging on expensive gowns, she took up sewing and found that she could make her own clothing for considerably less. In the times of quiet solitude that she spent stitching, she dreamed of the family she and George could spoil with funds she'd set aside. "I think of the days of peace," she wrote to George on June 10, 1864, "when little children's voices will call to us. I can hardly wait for my little boy and girl." In another letter she wrote to George about the prayers she said for a baby: "Autie, if God gives me children, I shall say to them: 'Emulate your father! I can give you no higher earthly example.'"[29]

Elizabeth knew that she and George would not be able to focus on their mutual desire for a family until the Civil War had ended. From mid-June through the end of October, 1864, they saw each other fewer than fifty times. Elizabeth was despondent over what felt like to her to be long periods of time apart, and wrote to a friend in Detroit about how frustrated she was by it: "It was never intended by the Creator that husband and wife should be separated," she noted sharply, "and so I am sometimes quite ready to rebel against this living alone like a little old maid."[30]

At one point her loneliness turned to horror when rumors circulated that George had been killed in battle.

It started with a newspaper story in late summer of 1864, which erroneously stated that he had died in a battle in Virginia. A paperboy on the corner near her boardinghouse in Washington was barking, "Custer killed! Read all about Custer being killed!" She was heartsick. When the Custers' family friend, congressman John Bingham, learned of the report, he rushed to the War Department to get confirmation. He was quickly informed that the newspapers were wrong and hurried off to Elizabeth's home to let her know.

"I found her pale and trembling and crying," Congressman Bingham wrote in his memoirs. "She was waiting for some word, and, seeing me, feared the worst. But when I told her, she broke down completely from relief and joy."[31]

In a letter dated October 28, 1864, the very-much-alive George invited Elizabeth to come and visit him at the camp where he was stationed near Martinsburg, Virginia. Elizabeth quickly accepted the invitation and hurried to meet the train that would take her to George. When Elizabeth arrived, she learned that George's brother Tom had joined the Michigan Brigade and was at the post as well. Tom was a handsome twenty-two-year-old lieutenant whose assignment was serving as aide-de-camp. Elizabeth and Tom were very close, and she was quite impressed with the respect he had for George. He politely yielded to his brother's authority and eagerly obeyed the commands he was given.[32]

For months Elizabeth followed George and his men from one camp setting to the next. She enjoyed the fast pace of army life and considered sleeping on the ground and living in a tent to be quite freeing. In a letter to her cousin,

Rebecca Richmond, she referred to a soldier's life as "glorious." She wrote that with each passing day, she and George grew closer to each other. She proclaimed in the same letter, "no happier woman lives than your cousin Libbie."[33]

Elizabeth left her beloved George and his division in February 1865 and returned to Washington. A week after her departure, the Michigan Brigade engaged the Rebel forces in battle at Waynesboro and in the Shenandoah Valley. While in Charlottesville, Virginia, George had happened onto a dispatch between Confederate generals Robert E. Lee and Jubal Early. The messages contained plans to attack Union general Philip Sheridan and his troops, located in Western Virginia. George and his men pursued General Early and thwarted their attempt.

George wrote to Elizabeth from the battlefield to let her know that she was ever present on his mind. "My Darling . . . I long for the return of peace. I look forward to our future with earnest hope. Our state may be far below our present one. We may not have the means for enjoyment we now possess, but we shall have enough to spare. Above all, we shall have each other. I think of you, even in the excitement of battle, and at night I dream of my darling."[34]

On April 9, 1865, the peace George and his Libbie longed for finally arrived. His part in Lee's surrender at Appomattox was noted in newspapers and magazines across the Eastern Seaboard. The division George was placed in charge of had stopped the fast-moving Confederate Army at Lynchburg Road, not far from the Appomattox Court House, and kept the Rebels from overtaking the area.

Elizabeth was extremely proud and cheerfully accepted the congratulations offered by adoring and grateful women in her sphere of influence.

George's commander, Philip Sheridan, echoed the sentiments of a grateful public in a letter to Elizabeth, dated April 10, 1865. The gift that accompanied the correspondence was confirmation that George was every bit the conquering hero she had come to idolize: "My Dear Madam, I respectfully present to you the small writing table on which the conditions for the surrender of the Confederate Army of Northern Virginia were written by Lieutenant General Grant, and permit me to say, Madam, that there is scarcely an individual in our service who has contributed more to bring about this desirable result than your very gallant husband."[35]

Elizabeth and George were reunited at a camp near Petersburg, Virginia. "His golden hair had grown past his shoulders," Elizabeth wrote to a friend. "He is tanned, but thin and worn. The most resplendent sight I've ever seen."[36]

CHAPTER FOUR

COMMON ENEMIES

Few living women can ride a horse equal to her, and but few better.

—GEORGE CUSTER'S THOUGHTS ABOUT ELIZABETH'S EQUESTRIAN SKILLS, 1866

A group of mounted Union officers rode onto the crest of a barren hill overlooking Fort Riley, Kansas, in January 1867. Captain Frederick Benteen was in the lead, his eyes sharp as an eagle's as he searched out the vast country ahead with exceeding care. The military outpost the soldiers were riding toward had been established to protect settlers and railroad workers from Indian attacks. Benteen and his company were going to reinforce that protection. He had led troops in the battle against Cheyenne leader Black Kettle and his braves on the Washita River (near what is now Cheyenne, Oklahoma) after the Civil War. As he was wont to remind his peers, "I struck the first blow in the Indian Wars . . ."[1]

In addition to his involvement at the start of the Indian wars, Benteen openly agreed with his superior officer, General Philip Sheridan—who had been named administrator over the Great Plains after the War Between the States—that the best way to defeat the Indians would

43

be to attack them during the winter months.[2] The Plains Indians depended heavily on their warrior ponies, which could easily outrun army horses and didn't need saddles and shoes to do their jobs. They required very little sustenance—no grain at all, just clumps of grass and very little water. The warrior ponies could also stand for hours without moving or neighing, which allowed their riders to easily sneak up on prey (deer, buffalo, etc.). However, winter was particularly hard on the animals because the ground was frozen. Finding any grass at all to eat under several layers of ice and snow was difficult, so in the winter season, the ponies were generally just skin and bones. Conversely, army horses were sturdy during the winter, having been fed with hearty rations of grain. Soldiers could ride into an Indian village, attack, and ride off, with little fear of being followed.[3]

Although Benteen shared his executive officer's views on when to engage the Indians in battle, and had proven his considerable soldiering skills and dedication to the Union cause, General Sheridan made George Custer commander of the cavalry at Fort Riley. Benteen, like many other cavalrymen—including Captain John Gresham, Major Marcus Reno, and Major Abner Dowling—resented George, who was one of the youngest decorated heroes of the Civil War, had attended West Point, and rode Thoroughbreds.[4] Rumor had it that he was conceited as a result of the accolades he had received and that his wife, Elizabeth, was just as haughty. She, too, was educated and had mingled with presidents, senators, and generals.

Benteen had not attended college and had an overall disdain for West Point graduates. His horse was not pedigreed, he'd received no special recognition for his soldiering during the war, and his wife was not socially connected.*

Benteen believed that answering to George would be difficult and that supporting his staff would be a daily struggle, but orders had been given.[5]

A freezing-cold wind tore through the acres of dried prairie grass around Benteen, and he pulled up the collar on his thick, wool coat to cover his neck. The soldiers riding beside him adjusted their caps and scarves to protect themselves from a light snow. The sabers affixed to their uniforms clinked against the stirrups of their saddles and mixed with the distant sound of railroad workers' hammers driving spikes into new tracks.

After several miles of riding, the first scattered structures of Fort Riley slid by Benteen and his men, gradually taking the form of a rugged thoroughfare that traveled through unpainted wooden buildings crowded absurdly into the midst of the open Kansas terrain. Benteen glanced back at the distance the cavalry had covered and squinted thoughtfully at the snow-covered plains.[6]

* After the surrender at Appomattox, Frederick Benteen was mustered into the 138th U.S. Colored Troops with very little fanfare. He then purchased a home in Atlanta and worked a small plantation with his wife and children. When the army was reconstructed in 1866, Benteen applied for a commission to serve on the frontier. In November of that year he was tendered a captain's commission with the 7th Cavalry.

On May 23, 1865, cheering throngs had gathered on either side of Pennsylvania Avenue in Washington, D.C. The War Between the States had ended at last, and soldiers, military leaders, and citizens from every state met at the country's capital to celebrate the conclusion of the bloody conflict. Dignitaries sat beneath flags emblazoned with the names of Union victories, and parade after parade of Northern troops marched proudly past the reviewing stand.[7]

George Custer was among the decorated cavalry leaders who led troops down the impossibly busy street. George's horse was excited by the shouts of praise for his rider, and he struggled to keep the animal from galloping away. Elizabeth, adorned in black-and-white taffeta and a black velvet riding cap with a scarlet feather, applauded George as he and the skittish steed trotted by her and the others. George's long yellow curls floated in the wind. He wore the full dress uniform of a brigadier general. Hundreds of women tossed bouquets of flowers into his path and sang "Hail to the Chief." It was an auspicious conclusion to his time leading a cavalry division.[8]

Soon after the ceremony in Washington, the Custers traveled to Louisiana, where George was to take command of a cavalry division organized to help restore parts of the Southwest still held by Rebel forces. As Elizabeth witnessed George's moving good-bye to his troops in the Michigan regiments, he became even more endearing to her. "I was too overcome . . . having seen the suffering on my husband's face," she wrote in her first book, *Tenting on the Plains*. "And I began to realize, as I watched this sad parting, the truth of what the General had been telling me; he held that no friendship was like that cemented by mutual danger on the battlefield. . . . Truly, Autie is the model of devotion and courage. Who dares imagine he was anything less? All the officers gathered about the General and wrung his hand in parting."[9]

Judge Bacon was apprehensive about Elizabeth's plans to accompany her husband to the still-war-torn Red River region in Louisiana. The cities and towns that lined the Red River in the northern portion of the state were leveled during the Union Army's efforts to capture Shreveport, the headquarters for the Confederate Army in the trans-Mississippi area during the Civil War. Judge Bacon was worried that it wasn't a safe place for wives of Union officers. As one of the last Confederate strongholds, the shipping port community was overrun with carpetbaggers, lawbreakers, and hostile Rebel soldiers who were angry about the outcome of the war and steadfast in holding their ground. The judge hoped Elizabeth would return to Monroe and live with him and her stepmother until George settled at a more congenial post.

"I'm going with Autie," Elizabeth told her father. "I'm always going to follow him wherever he's ordered, if I can. I've made up my mind to do that."[10]

Elizabeth enjoyed the time she was able to spend with George en route to his first assignment since the end of the Civil War. The pair traveled from Washington by train and then by steamer to their destination. George was happy to have Elizabeth by his side, and he often told her so. "It was a curious trip that journey up the Red River," Elizabeth recalled in her memoirs. "We saw the dull, brownish-red water from the clay bed and banks mingling with the clearer current of the Mississippi long before we entered the mouth of the Red River. We had a delightful journey; but I don't know why, except that youth, health, and buoyant spirits rise superior to everything."[11]

George and Elizabeth's relationship grew on the journey, and each learned a bit more about the other. During one of their many conversations about his current orders, however, Elizabeth sensed there was something George wasn't telling her. When pressed, he finally shared the extent of the job he had been asked to do. Not only was he to lead his division through Northern Louisiana, but also on into Texas, and possibly Mexico.[12] George confessed that the reason he hadn't told her everything prior to leaving Michigan was because he thought she would change her mind about going with him, and that they would float "southward by floods of feminine tears." Stalwart Elizabeth assured him there was no place she'd rather be than by his side.[13]

When their steamer docked in New Orleans, the Custers decided to stay on a few days as a delayed honeymoon. The couple took long walks through the French Quarter, enjoyed French cuisine, and visited many shops. George, who Elizabeth noted in her journal was "tired and worn prematurely old after his years of fighting," was reinvigorated by spending this time with his wife. He was excited to return to work.

After a few days, General Sheridan summoned George to his headquarters to discuss the possible campaign into

Mexico, and to select a staff that would serve under him. Among the eight officers George was allowed to pick for his staff was his brother Tom.[14]

Elizabeth, George, and his personnel moved on to Alexandria, Louisiana. The Custers' temporary home and headquarters for the westward fighting division was a large white house that had lofty rooms and two wings. When George wasn't organizing and unifying a division of men (selected from both the North and South) out of reluctant, rebellious recruits that hadn't ever been in battle, he and Elizabeth were horseback riding.[15] They felt isolated from the rest of the world as they galloped through the valley beyond the busy makeshift post where they had been assigned. "We sometimes rode for miles," Elizabeth wrote in her journal, "along the country roads, between hedges of Osage-orange on one side, and a double white rose on the other, growing fifteen feet high. The dew enhanced the fragrance, and a lavish profusion was displayed by nature in that valley, which was a constant delight to us. Sometimes my husband and I remained out very late, loath to come back. . . ."[16]

George struggled with insubordination among the troops he commanded. They willfully disobeyed orders and robbed individuals and homes in the area they were supposed to be protecting. When George dealt harshly with the rogue soldiers, the men he disciplined threatened his life, and Elizabeth pleaded with him to protect himself from attack. George refused, insisting he would not give in to intimidation. "Still seeing what I suffered from anxiety," Elizabeth later noted, "he made one concession, and consented, after much imploring, to put a pistol under his pillow." Months later she learned that George had never loaded the gun. He only wanted to ease her worries.[17]

After six weeks, George's commitment to the betterment of his division saw results. The troops had stopped fighting against one another and protesting the training they were made to go through. They were a cohesive unit of 5,000 men, ready to move out when ordered.

In late July 1865, George received news that he was to lead his division west to Texas. A special spring wagon, once used as a cavalry combat vehicle, was made ready for Elizabeth. The wagon had a place for her to sleep, a dressing room, curtains, adjustable seats, and a rainproof rubber roof. Elizabeth was grateful to George for such considerations, but informed him that she would not take advantage of his thoughtfulness. She planned to ride horseback for much of the trip—just like the others in the outfit. The many long rides she had taken with her husband while in Louisiana had prepared her for the grueling journey.[18]

Although Elizabeth did not openly complain, she did note in her journal that "little measure of comfort was to be found in the overland travel."

"A short time after we set out," she later wrote, "we left the Red River, with its fertile plantations, and entered a pine forest on the table-land, through which our route lay for a hundred and fifty miles. A great portion of the higher ground was sterile, and the forest much of the way was thinly inhabited. We had expected to hire a room in any farmhouse at which we halted at the end of each day's journey, and have the privilege of sleeping in a bed. Camping on the ground was an old story to me, [. . .] but the prospect of using the bosom of mother Earth as a nesting-place for the coming thirty years, we were willing to improve any opportunity to be comfortable when we could."[19]

Elizabeth was concerned about being a burden to George. She did not want to slow down the march or stop the expedition to tend to her needs. She got herself up and ready each morning, taking just seven minutes to bathe, dress, and do her hair. George was impressed with her discipline and often bragged about how adaptable she was to the other officers and their wives.[20]

According to Elizabeth's memoirs, George was very attentive to her on the journey. He would roll up his overcoat for her to use as a pillow, bring her water, and consistently praise her for her veteran-like behavior.[21] She looked out for George, too, cutting his hair and keeping it short so he would be cooler. She frequently commended him for his bravery and leadership. "There was no one whose temper and strength were not tried to the uttermost, except my husband," she recalled years later. "His seeming indifference to the excessive heat, his having long before conquered thirst, his apparent unconsciousness of the stings or bites of insects, were powerful aids in encountering those suffocating days."[22]

After marching fifteen miles a day for thirteen days, Elizabeth, George, and the other troops arrived at the headquarters for the Federal Army of Observation in Hempstead, Texas. General Sheridan and his staff met Custer and his division at the post shortly after arrival. He was impressed with how well George had handled the rowdy recruits he had been assigned. There had been no trouble on the march, and the troops showed great promise toward being able to achieve their objective. As a result, Sheridan placed George in charge of all cavalry operations in Texas. Much to George's disappointment, being placed in charge of all the cavalry did not come with a pay raise. According to Elizabeth's journal, George's pay was barely enough to take care of himself adequately while in the field, so having her with him was an added expense—albeit a necessary one, in his estimation. There were no extra quarters available for officers' wives and no allotment for food beyond the daily meals served at the mess hall. In addition to that, officers were generally expected to entertain fellow officers and staff, supplying them with liquor and cigars. The army did not compensate anyone for those costs.[23]

The couple lived on a little more than $150 a month. George had opportunities for earning additional income "in land, or cotton, or horses, or in buying government claims," Elizabeth wrote to her parents in October 1865. "But he feels that so long as the government needs his active services, he should not invest."[24]

In spite of her affluent upbringing, Elizabeth was able to live on very little; George, on the other hand, liked cigars, fine liquor, and gambling. The money the two had managed to save after they were first married was disappearing as a result of George's indulgences. Since the end of the war, George had taken funds out of their savings to pay for gambling debts, the purchase of new racing ponies, food for the numerous hounds he owned, and so forth. As a result, the money was slowly dwindling away.[25]

Although she was envious at times because she had to share George with his numerous dogs, Elizabeth was quite fond of the animals. "A dog is so human to me," she wrote in a letter home, "and dogs have been my husband's chosen friends so many years, I cannot look upon the common cur with indifference."[26]

From Hempstead, the Custers and his troops pressed on to a post near Austin. In the beginning, Elizabeth thought Austin was an inhospitable place. There were no railroads, bandits and horse thieves roamed unopposed over the area, and former Confederate soldiers resisted change and refused to treat black men and women as free people. While George and his division tried to instill some order, Elizabeth made the military quarters, where they resided with his staff, a home. The quarters consisted of a two-story building with two long, one-story wings attached. The Custers enjoyed a view of Austin and the snowy hills beyond from their upstairs parlor, and warmed themselves at the giant fireplaces featured in every room.[27]

The challenges involved with being the commander of an outpost were great, but George was equal to the task. Off duty he and Elizabeth hosted dances and hunting expeditions and explored their surroundings on horseback. Elizabeth noted in her memoirs that they found the country around Austin delightful. "The roads were smooth and the surface rolling," she elaborated. "Indeed, there was one hill, called Mount Brunnel, where we had picnics and enjoyed the fine view, far and near, taking one of the bands of the regular regiments from the North that joined us soon after our arrival. Mount Brunnel was so steep we had to dismount and climb a part of the distance. The band played the 'Anvil Chorus,' and the sound descended through the valley grandly."[28]

George took long rides alone, as well, leading his horse south across the Colorado River to the Deaf and Dumb Asylum that was located near Austin, Texas, to visit with the students in attendance there. Elizabeth knew of his great love for children and how helpful it was for him and the boys and girls at the school to spend time together. George was awestruck by the way the children communicated. The sign language they used was quick and fluid. The general picked up the language easily and learned how to sign along with the rest of the students. He became a much-loved figure in the classroom. Each time he visited he brought gifts, including sheet music, maps, and books. George had hopes that sign language might possibly be useful in dealing with the Plains Indians.[29]

The hours George spent with the students served to remind him of how much he and Elizabeth wanted children of their own. She prayed for a baby, and that George would commit himself to the same prayer, and to the church. "Oh, how I hope for a child that I might try and make it a cornerstone in the great church of God," she recalled, petitioning the Lord in October 1864.[30]

The soirees the Custers held at the army garrison near Austin helped to take Elizabeth's mind off of her overwhelming, but unfulfilled, desire for children. The Custers' social events were always well attended by the men at the post. Among the officers who participated in the festivities was Captain Thomas Weir, a graduate of the University of Michigan and a veteran of the Civil War. His regiment was assigned to Reconstruction duty in 1865, and he had previously served under George while in the Southeast.

Both George and Elizabeth found Weir to be a charming, extremely likable fellow. He had an intellectual side that set him apart from his fellow soldiers, and striking features that made him appealing to many women. His vice was alcohol, which he frequently consumed in great quantities. He and Elizabeth enjoyed many stimulating conversations, and it was obvious to other officers with the 7th Cavalry that the pair was smitten with one another. When talking with the officers, George spoke disapprovingly of how his wife was perhaps overly friendly, but countered his remarks with praise for her "generous heart and ability to make friends easily."[31]

In February 1866, after five months of service in the Southwest, George was relieved of duty, joining the ranks of thousands of other soldiers being mustered out of the military. The situation had stabilized in Louisiana and Texas, and the threat of war with Ferdinand Maximilian, the self-proclaimed emperor of Mexico* and his imperial troops had been resolved.[32]

---

* Backed by Napoleon III, Maximilian had allowed French troops to move into Mexico and to assemble at the border between Mexico and the United States. The plan was to take U.S. territory. Benito Juarez's liberal Mexican forces, opposed to Maximilian and Napoleon, put an end to the occupation and planned invasion.

George and Elizabeth returned to Michigan. Like many other officers at the time, George lost his wartime rank when the military began downsizing. He was now only a captain in the United States Cavalry, but the citizens of Monroe gave the Boy General and Elizabeth, his lady fair, a hero's welcome. The couple stayed with Judge Bacon and his wife during their visit, and there was a continuous stream of friends and family parading in and out of the home. Everyone wanted to know about life on the Great Plains and the Custers' future plans. Many business opportunities were offered to George. Corporation owners and Wall Street brokers encouraged him to capitalize on his name and reputation and lend them both to various products and services. Civic organizations wanted him to make a run for Congress or for governor. The promise of financial independence for him and his wife tempted the twenty-six-year-old Civil War veteran. "For you and you alone I long to become wealthy," he told Elizabeth, "not for the wealth alone, but for the power it brings. I am willing to make any honorable sacrifice."[33]

In early March, George decided to go to Washington and New York to further explore some of the career options that had been presented to him. Elizabeth reluctantly agreed to stay behind in Monroe. George spent a great deal of time with entrepreneurs and established politicians discussing what ventures he might pursue. In between business meetings, artists and photographers flocked to him, pleading for a picture or a chance to cast his image in bronze. His social calendar was just as full. He attended parties, operas, and the theater, and on more than one occasion, he escorted a young actress named Margaret Mitchell to the events. Margaret was the most popular actress of the time, blonde, beautiful, and highly sought after.

George was forthcoming with Elizabeth about his association with Margaret and insisted the relationship was purely platonic. In a letter to his wife, dated April 1, 1866, George informed Elizabeth that he had been keeping company with the actress. "I called on Maggie Mitchell, at the house where she lives with her mother, a handsome residence on 54th Street, near Fifth Avenue," he wrote. "A delightful visit. Her manners are so pleasing, her conversation so refined, you would not suppose she had been on stage."[34]

Some of the women George kept company with were not quite as respectable as Margaret. On April 3, 1866, George wrote to Elizabeth about his night on the town with a few West Point officers and ladies they met on the street. "After the theatre," George shared with his wife, "several of us went on an expedition in search of fun—visited several shooting galleries, pretty-girl-waitress saloons . . . 'Nymphes du Pave' they are called. Sport alone was our object. At no time did I forget you."[35]

None of the business ventures posed to George held the same interest for him as being a soldier. In a letter to Elizabeth, he wrote that "the sound of the horse's hoofs on this road makes me think of cavalry on the march." George decided that he would hold out for another command rather than abandon the military.

Elizabeth supported her husband. "If you want a regiment of cavalry and bugles blowing, that's exactly what I want for you," she assured him.[36]

On May 18, 1866, Judge Bacon died at the age of sixty-eight, after a bout with cholera. His death shifted Elizabeth's focus from her husband's future endeavors to planning her father's funeral. Elizabeth and her stepmother had been by Judge Bacon's side when he died. Before he closed his eyes forever, he spoke of his daughter and George. Elizabeth recorded his statements in her journal: "Elizabeth was married entirely to her own satisfaction and to mine. No man could wish for a son-in-law more highly thought of."[37]

Elizabeth was heartsick over her father's death. In a letter to a family friend, written shortly after Judge Bacon's funeral, she noted how their house was "not the same. . . . Mother is visiting in Clinton; I do not think she will ever be strong enough to keep house again. I should be far more miserable but for Armstrong's care. He keeps me out of doors as much as he can. I do not wear deep mourning. He is opposed to it."[38]

After making generous provisions for his wife, Elizabeth's father left the bulk of his holdings and estate to his daughter. George tried to help Elizabeth deal with the loss by taking his wife on a variety of trips. They went to Detroit and Toledo, visited with friends, and rode their horses across the Ohio countryside. In time the pain lessened.

George's desire to return to active duty prompted him to consider joining the Mexican Army. The country was occupied by French and Austrian troops who wanted to claim the land for themselves. After learning that General Sheridan was a part of Mexico's campaign, and that there was a great need for cavalry leadership, George wanted to commit his service to the fight. General Ulysses Grant wrote a letter on George's behalf to the office at the Headquarters of Armies of the United States. (At this time George was a captain in the 5th U.S. Calvary, his volunteer commission in the regular army having expired earlier in the year.) The letter requested that George be given a year's leave of absence so that he could aid President Juarez in his objective.[39]

General Grant's request to the government on behalf of George was denied. Political leaders like Secretary of State William Seward did not want U.S. troops involved in Mexico's affairs. He wanted the country to maintain an air of neutrality. And General Philip Sheridan had other plans for George—plans that involved watching over the territory west of the Mississippi. In July 1866, Congress passed the Army Act, creating a postwar army that authorized 54,000 troops to work toward three basic missions: Reconstruction of the South; defense of the seacoasts; and protection of the Western frontier. George was to be a key player in the latter.

Finally, George was appointed lieutenant colonel of the 7th Cavalry and ordered to an outpost in the Kansas territory. His job was to deal with the Indians who were harassing settlers and attacking surveying and construction parties working for the Kansas-Pacific Railroad. George was excited and quickly found the location where he was to report for duty in the atlas. As Elizabeth wrote in her memoirs, "It was a comparatively old post, and the railroad was within ten miles of the Government reservation."[40]

After a stop at Leavenworth to lay in supplies for the trip in October 1866, the Custers and members of their party proceeded "over the hills and far away," as Elizabeth put it.[41] They set out for the West in October 1866. George's Thoroughbred horses and several of his dogs accompanied the pair on their journey. As they pulled out of Leavenworth, the last words Elizabeth's father had said to her before he died in May 1866 echoed in her head: "Daughter, continue to do as you have done; follow Armstrong everywhere."[42]

The trek over the Plains was both difficult and invigorating for Elizabeth. In letters home to her family, she described the pros and cons of overland travel. "I am never happier than when sleeping in a tent," she confessed to her aunt. "It is so comfortable. Storms are our only trouble—thunder, lightning, freshets, wind. But our tent is well staked. . . . There are some drawbacks to Kansas, but it is a fine spot to begin life in, with good farming land. There is trouble with Indians, within twenty miles from us coming down from the North. A part of the regiment is still in camp, so that I am not afraid, near such a large body of men."[43]

When the Custers arrived at Fort Riley, General William Tecumseh Sherman, commanding general of the army, was on hand to welcome them to the post. Elizabeth had expected the garrison to be surrounded by stone walls, with "turrets for sentinels, and a deep moat."[44] But the troop station was nothing more than a collection of wooden buildings set about a parade ground. Nearby were a few workshops, barracks, barns for hay, and stables for horses. Beyond, an immense, empty, rolling plain stretched to the horizon. There were no trees in sight except a thin line of cottonwoods along a stream near the fort.

Elizabeth and George settled into a large house built for the commanding officer. "There were parlors on one side, whose huge folding doors were flung open, and made our few articles of furniture look lonely and meager," Elizabeth wrote in her memoirs.[45] George was eager to get to work organizing the 7th Cavalry and training the troops. With the exception of Tom Custer and Thomas Weir, most of the soldiers were new to the army, and new to life in the unsettled Western country. George had four months in which to get his regiment into shape.

General Winfield Scott Hancock, commander of all the troops in the region, had planned a military campaign for the spring of 1867. He informed his officers that Cheyenne Indian leaders like Pawnee Killer, Lame Deer, and Runs Fearless were upset over the invasion of their land and did not trust the United States government. Hancock felt that the only way to combat these Cheyenne Indians and their followers was to take a strong force of infantry, cavalry, and artillery out after them. Hancock hoped that the action would scare the Indians into making peace and settling down on the reservations they had been relegated to. Eight captains were appointed to report to George for orders, and among them was Frederick Benteen.

CHAPTER FIVE

MISSING ELIZABETH

*Daughter, marrying into the army, you will be poor
always; but I count it infinitely preferable to riches with
inferior society.*

—JUDGE BACON TO ELIZABETH CUSTER, 1866

George Custer raced his stallion, Jack, at full speed over
the seemingly limitless grass-covered plateau miles away
from the main entrance of Fort Riley, Kansas. The foam-
flecked animal was inches behind Elizabeth and her fast
horse, Custis Lee. Both riders urged their horses on to even
greater speed, the cold wind biting at their smiling faces.

George steered his ride along the foot of a high hill.
Reaching a steep decline, he abruptly brought his horse to
a halt. Elizabeth, riding sidesaddle and dressed in a black
riding skirt, uniform jacket, and a light-blue felt hat with a
leather visor in front known as an excelsior hat, pulled farther ahead of her husband. Quickly looking around, George
turned Jack in the direction of a narrow trail through a flinty
apron of rocks. He followed the crude path as it wound
around the hill and then suddenly dropped back down,
coming out the other side of the steep decline in front of

Elizabeth. She waved playfully at him. The horses found their rhythm and broke into a smooth gallop. Elizabeth glanced over at George and giggled like a little girl. The two rode on toward a distant, tumbled pile of thunderheads, sooty black at their base and white as whipped cream where they towered against the dome of sky.

They slowed their horses and stopped next to a cluster of rocks. George dismounted and helped Elizabeth down from her mount. Draping their arms around each other, they stood quietly, staring at the land stretched out before them. "The prairie was worth looking over," Elizabeth noted in her memoirs, "because it changed like the sea." "People thought of the deep-grass as brown, but in the spring it could look almost anything else," she added, "purple, or gold, or red, or any kind of blue. Often when cloud shadows crossed the long swells, the whole prairie stirred, and seemed to mold and flow, as if it breathed." [1] In late January 1867, however, the terrain the Custers admired was winter-defeated, lightless and without color.

George loosened the hold he had on Elizabeth, and she noticed his expression change subtly. As post commander he needed to return to his duties. The responsibilities of coordinating and training more than 960 enlisted men were daunting, but the twenty-seven-year-old was committed to the task. The occasional outing with Elizabeth gave him incentive to carry on, and gave her a chance to explore the countryside, blissfully unaware of anything other than her husband. "It was delightful ground to ride over Fort Riley," she remembered years later. "Ah! What happy days they were, for at that time I had not the slightest realization of what Indian warfare was, and consequently no dread."[2]

George removed a bugle from his saddlebag and gave it a long blast. Several of his greyhound dogs responded to the sound and came running. They eagerly danced around the couple, waiting for their master to lead the way. Elizabeth and George rode slowly back to the post. After an hour the sight of the United States flag waving over the barracks came into view. Over time the persistent wind had torn the colors into ribbons. By the time George and Elizabeth arrived at the camp, the gleam of fading, lemon-yellow sunlight that had stained the sky above the western horizon was matched by the glow of the rising moon.[3]

A great swarming of men and horses made their way from one end of the post to the other and back again. Some were on duty, and others were en route to the trader's store for a drink. Alcohol was never in short supply, and the soldiers were prone to overindulge, particularly on payday.[4] Boredom, fear, and loneliness were the chief reasons for drunkenness, and drinking wasn't relegated to a particular rank. George had struggled with alcohol until he had married Elizabeth. His conversion to Christianity and his wife's influence kept him sober. Remembering how it made him physically ill made a difference as well, and he preached temperance to his troops. Elizabeth noted in her memoirs that it was difficult for George to keep his men from drinking. "His own greatest battles were not fought in the tented field," she recalled. "[H]is most glorious combats were those waged in daily, hourly fights on a more hotly contested field than was ever known in common warfare."[5]

George permitted his staff to drink alcohol in moderation. He and Elizabeth would yield to those who enjoyed a glass of wine with friends to toast a promotion or birth. The Custers, however, would not partake. Elizabeth worried that the officers' appetite for alcoholic beverages might lead to impaired judgment if they came under attack by the Indians. George assured his wife that he had the utmost confidence in his staff and their ability to sober up quickly. "It was on the battlefield, when all faced death together, where the truest affection was formed among soldiers," he told her.[6]

It was during a social occasion where alcohol was being served at the Custers' quarters on January 30, 1867, that Frederick Benteen first reported to George. Benteen noted in his memoirs that the tension between the two men was "quite palpable." George was surrounded by his loyal staff, among them his brother Tom, Myles Moylan, and George Yates, the latter two having served with George during the Civil War. Also present were Algernon E. Smith, an old sailor, and Thomas Weir, a veteran of George's staff in Texas. Benteen was reserved, but respectful. He saluted George, and the commanding officer returned the address. The men reminisced briefly about their days with the Union Army.[7]

One of George's men mentioned that Benteen was not a West Point graduate, nor was he an educated man, and outside of the military, he had no profession. Benteen was annoyed by the remarks, but maintained his composure.

George then asked Elizabeth to bring him the scrapbook that he had kept from his time in the Civil War, and she complied. The veterans pored over the tome, recalling various victories. George's pride disgusted Benteen, and he scowled at the young leader's tales. The conversation grew heated when George produced a copy of the farewell address he had given his troops at the end of the war. Benteen snapped at George, insisting that there were numerous generals much more skilled who had offered better speeches, and that one such man was Brigadier General James Wilson. (Benteen had fought beside Wilson during the Civil War.[8]) Through gritted teeth, Benteen began reciting a portion of Wilson's farewell address.

Elizabeth was a bit taken aback by the gruff, near-hostile turn of the discussion. Lieutenant Thomas Weir reached out to steady her. She gently leaned into his supportive arms. Years after Benteen had first seen Elizabeth and Thomas together at the Custers' home, he claimed the pair was more than just friends. Benteen did not miss the subtle exchange between Thomas and Elizabeth; in fact, it sparked his suspicions. Elizabeth then interrupted the officer, and in an effort to defuse the tension, offered to give him a tour of their quarters. Benteen declined and asked to be dismissed to continue on with his duties. George granted his request, and the men parted company with a salute.[9]

George was well aware that not everyone liked him, but this had no bearing on the job he had been assigned to do: to ensure that his troops were trained for combat. He expected a lot from his regiment, and regularly drove the soldiers, who on average earned about $13 a month, to their endurance and beyond. The soldiers participated in daily target practice with their Spencer repeating rifles and Colt Army revolvers; performed horseback riding drills; took lessons in tactics and regimental discipline; and learned basic first aid. The work was tedious and exhausting. Disillusioned by the grueling pace of military life on the frontier, more than eighty enlisted men deserted before they had even served a full year at Fort Riley.[10]

Those men who chose not to desert but still refused to obey orders were sent to the guardhouse. The facility was located outside the garrison and could hold a number of inmates. Disobedient soldiers interned there were nervous that the stockade would be overtaken by hostile Indians and that they would have no way of defending themselves. Some tried to escape before their fears could be realized.[11] Elizabeth described a unique escape in her journal in the winter of 1867:

For several nights, at one time, strange sounds for such a place issued from the walls," she wrote. "Religion in the noisiest form seemed to have taken up its permanent abode there, and for three hours at a time, singing, shouting, and loud praying went on. There was every appearance of a revival among those trespassers. The officer of the day, in making his rounds, had no comment to pass upon this remarkable transition from card playing and wrangling; he was doubtless relieved to hear the voice of the exhorters as he visited the guard [house] and indulged in the belief that the prisoners were out of mischief."

On the contrary, this vehement attack of religion covered up the worst sort of roguery. Night after night they had been digging tunnels under the stone foundation-walls, removing boards and cutting beams in the floor, and to deaden the sound of the pounding and digging, some of their numbers were told to sing, pray, and shout.

One morning the guard opened the door of the rooms in which the prisoners had been confined, and they were empty! Even two that wore ball and chains for serious offenses had in some manner managed to knock them off, as all had swum the Smoky Hill River, and they were never again heard from.[12]

George needed to minimize the desertions, get the prisoners in the stockade back in line, and have the 7th Cavalry fully trained by the spring of 1867, in order to be prepared for the planned campaign against the Cheyenne. "We'll take a strong force of infantry, cavalry, and artillery out after them," General Winfield Scott Hancock informed George. "We'll try to scare them so they'll make peace and settle down on the reservation which has been assigned to them. If they won't, we'll destroy them."[13]

George had mixed feelings about the Indians. Their ruthless attacks on army troopers traveling the Plains prompted him to refer to Native Americans as "blood-thirsty savages." But he was also torn between a soldier's hatred of an "enemy" and admiration for why that enemy was fighting him. "If I were an Indian, I often think that I would greatly prefer to cast my lot among those of my people who adhere to the free open plains, rather than submit to the confined limits of a reservation, there to be the recipient of the blessed benefits of civilization, with its vices thrown in without stint or measure."[14]

While George worked steadily to train the soldiers at Fort Riley to be the best on the Plains, Elizabeth lamented the fact that he would soon be leaving her for potentially hazardous duty. She was frightened for him and sad that she couldn't go with him on the campaign. "My husband tried to keep my spirits up," Elizabeth wrote in her memoirs, "by reminding me that the council to be held with the chiefs of the war-like tribes, when they reached that part of the country infested with the marauding Indians, was something he hoped might result in our speedy reunion."[15]

The Custers sought relief from the stress of their pending separation by hosting social events for George's staff and their families. Elizabeth held dinner parties, and George invited his officers over to play poker. Benteen attended the soirees, but was highly critical of the couple's behavior. He claimed that Elizabeth "presided with correctness over the army wives and had no scruples about favoring the wives of her husband's allies and snubbing those of his enemies."[16] He also maintained that George was an "inveterate and inferior gambler" and that his habit was obvious.[17]

In writing to his friend, Theodore Goldin, in late February 1867, Benteen described a time when George lost big at cards. Benteen had joined George, Tom Custer, Lieutenant Myles Moylan, and Thomas Weir for an evening of five-hand poker with dime ante and table stakes. At one point in the game, only three players remained—George, Thomas Weir, and Benteen. Believing he had a hand that would make up for the money he had lost early in the night, George suggested the stakes be raised to $2.50. Everyone agreed. George's bad luck didn't change. By the first morning light, Benteen had won a considerable amount. Thomas Weir had lost more than a month's salary ($150.00), and George's debt was nearly double that amount. Neither had the money to cover their bets but promised to pay Benteen as soon as they could. Benteen claimed he had never received what he was owed from either of the men.[18]

As the time neared for George and his troops to leave the post on their expedition with General Hancock, Elizabeth became more anxious. The Fetterman Massacre of December 1866 was fresh on her mind: Eighty soldiers led by Captain William J. Fetterman had been ambushed and killed near Fort Phil Kearny (in what is now Wyoming) when they had left the post to go to the aid of a woodcutting party. More than 1,900 Sioux, Cheyenne, and Apache warriors had taken part in the slaughter.[19]

Eight companies, consisting of infantry and artillery soldiers numbering more than 1,400 men, would be accompanying George on the expedition, but Elizabeth believed it was too few. Other wives at the camp felt the same way. "No one can enumerate the terrors, imaginary and real, that filled the hearts of women on the border in those desperate days," Elizabeth wrote in her memoirs. "The buoyancy of my husband had only momentary effect in the last hours of his stay . . . such partings are a torture that is difficult even to refer to. My husband added another struggle to my lot by imploring me not to let him see the tears that he knew, for his sake, I could keep back until he was out of sight."[20]

In late March 1867, General Hancock, George, and eight companies of troops marched out of Fort Riley toward Fort Larned. A meeting between the army officers and the Cheyenne chiefs to negotiate the transfer of the Indians to the reservation was scheduled for April 10. The members of the 7th Cavalry arrived at the post on April 7 and helped to get the camp ready to receive the Indian council.[21] The day before the meeting was to take place, a blizzard blanketed the fort and the surrounding plains. The Cheyenne leaders not only refused to meet on the designated date because of the frigid weather, but they also expressed their irritation at the army for sending such a large expedition in the first place. General Hancock explained that he and his troops had come only to promote peace, but the Indians didn't believe him.[22]

George was not surprised that the Indians had postponed the council. During his time on the frontier, he had come to realize that no Indian was in a hurry to adopt the white man's manner of life. "In making this change," George wrote in his journal, "the Indian has to sacrifice all that is dear to his heart; he abandons the only mode of life in which he can be a warrior and win triumphs and honors worthy to be sought after. . . ."[23]

General Hancock twice rescheduled the meeting between the military leaders and Plains Indians chiefs, and each time, the date was ignored. Henry Morton Stanley and Theodore R. Davis, two journalists traveling with the cavalry, reported on how frustrated the general was that the Indians had repeatedly failed to show. Readers of *Harper's Weekly*, the *Missouri Democrat*, and the *New York Herald* were informed of George's opinion that the Indians were more frightened than belligerent.[24] General Hancock didn't agree. He viewed their behavior as a "commencement of war." He ordered Custer to take his troops and track the fugitives down.[25]

Back at Fort Riley, Elizabeth attended church to pray for the safe return of her husband and the other members of the 7th Cavalry. A small regiment of men had been left behind to guard the nearly deserted post. There were only two women at the camp besides Elizabeth. They longed for God to protect their loved ones and lived in fear that their petitions would not be answered. They ached for word from their husbands that all was well with them, but none came.[26]

In addition to her concern for George, a distant grass fire—sparked by lightning—was spreading across the prairie, inching its way toward the fort. There was no time for the soldiers to fight the blaze by burning a section of ground between the camp and the approaching fire. "In an incredibly short time we were overshadowed with a dark cloud of smoke," Elizabeth wrote in her memoirs. "There were no screams, nor cries, simply silent terror and shivering of horror, as we women huddled together to watch the remorseless fiend advancing with what appeared to be inevitable annihilation of the only shelter we had. Every woman's thoughts turned to her natural protector, now far away. . . ."[27] Using blankets, gunnysacks, and sheets, columns of stalwart soldiers beat the flames back. The fire danced around the post and continued on over the flat plains.

It would be weeks before news of the life-threatening fire would reach George. Although Elizabeth wrote to her husband daily, the letters could not catch up with him as he pursued bands of Cheyenne, Arapaho, Kiowa, and Comanche Indians north. By mid-April 1867, George and his troops had arrived at a stagecoach stop called Lookout Station, fifteen miles west of Fort Hays, in western Kansas. The trail of Indians they had been following led them to the location. At first the stop seemed to be deserted, but upon further inspection, George discovered that the people who had lived and worked at the depot had been brutally murdered and their bodies set on fire. The 7th Cavalry searched for weeks for the Indian offenders and found only more burned-down stage stations and slaughtered homesteaders. General Hancock was furious. He ordered George to continue to track the Indians, to kill them when he found them, and in between, to incinerate any abandoned Indian village they came upon.[28]

Before George and his men could go any farther, they needed to stock up on supplies. They held their position at Fort Hays, awaiting fresh horses, feed for the animals, and food for the field. George quickly sent for Elizabeth to join him at the post. On May 4, 1867, he wrote to tell her, "You will be delighted with the country." He added, "Bring a good supply of butter, one hundred pounds or more; three or four cans of lard; vegetables—potatoes, onions, and carrots. You will need calico dresses, and a few white ones. Oh, we will be so, so happy."[29]

Elizabeth and George were reunited for only a brief time at Fort Hays. The camp was primitive, but there was no trouble in or around the post during their visit. The couple enjoyed more than a week together. On June 1, 1867, George departed on a scouting expedition for wanted Indians along the Platte River.[30] He led the expedition, which included not only members of the 7th Cavalry, but also a column of 350 infantry troops and twenty wagons.[31] He left Elizabeth behind at Fort Hays, where he believed she would be safe.

George's key role in the expedition infuriated Benteen, who was already annoyed that Elizabeth had joined him at the new command post. Not only did he feel he was infinitely more qualified to command the scouting party, but he also longed to see his own wife, Kate, who was expecting their second child. Kate and their daughter were living at Fort Harker, Kansas, eighty miles east of Fort Hays. George chose Thomas Weir to remain in command at the post, promoting him from first lieutenant to captain in the process.[32]

George overlooked the grumbling and complaining from Benteen for the time being in order to focus on preparations for the long journey ahead. He kissed his wife good-bye and headed out. George was to lead his men to the headwaters of the Republican River, touch the Platte River at Fort Sedgwick—where he would be resupplied—and then move southward to Fort Wallace on the Smoky Hill River before returning to Fort Hays.[33]

While on the trail, dissatisfaction among the ranks raised its ugly head. The troops were tired, sick of being on the move, and drinking was once again on the rise. George was unable to persuade the men to abandon the habit. It wasn't until a popular, well-liked officer with the 7th Cavalry got drunk and then shot and killed himself that the troops changed their ways. George wrote about the incident in his memoirs on June 8, 1867: "But for intemperance Colonel Cooper would have been a useful and accomplished officer, a brilliant and most comparable gentleman. He leaves a young wife, shortly to become a mother. I thank God my darling wife will never know anxiety through intemperance on my part. Would I could fly to her now . . . but wise providence decrees all."[34]

The problem with drinking had subsided in the unit, but desertion was on the rise. Apprehensive about marching farther into hostile territory, thirty-five soldiers decided to leave their post in a single day. George wrote to Elizabeth, saying that "severe and summary measures must be taken." He directed his officers to shoot down the deserters as they fled the camp. A few men were killed, and many others were wounded. George felt the extreme measures were necessary to show other troops that such treasonous acts would result in harsh punishment. "The effect was all that could be desired," he shared with Elizabeth. "There was not another desertion as long as I remained in command."[35]

Elizabeth's letters, sent along with every passing stage, finally reached George on the outskirts of Fort McPherson. He barely had time to read them before being summoned to a rendezvous with Sioux Indian leaders on the Southern Plains. George's meeting with the Indians at their request resulted in their agreeing to relocate to a reservation in the coming days. When William Tecumseh Sherman, commander of the Division of Missouri from 1866 to 1868, arrived on the scene in Nebraska, he was not convinced the Indians would follow through. Frustrated by the unsuccessful attempts to move various Plains Indian tribes onto reservations, and under pressure from Washington to stop the killing of pioneers, Sherman ordered George to "clean out the renegades."[36]

Several weeks had passed since George and Elizabeth had been together. Elizabeth kept herself busy with the demands of being an officer's wife and upholding the social obligations that would bolster morale and maintain a sense of hope. During the tea parties and dinners she hosted, she would share stories with the camp inhabitants about the emigrants she and George had met en route to the fort. Heavy spirits were lifted by Elizabeth's recollections of life on the frontier with George. "How well I remember the long wait we made on one of the staircases of the Capitol at Washington, above which hung then the great picture by Leutze, *Westward the Course of Empire Takes Its Way*," she noted. "We little thought then, hardly more than girl and boy as we were, that our lives would drift over the country which the admirable picture represents. . . . The picture made a great impression on us. How much deeper the impression, though, had we known that we were to live out the very scene depicted."[37]

Even in the midst of organizing and implementing a search of the country around the fork of the Republican River, then pressing onward to Fort Sedgwick, Nebraska, to receive additional orders, George had but one thing on his mind, and that was completing his assignment so he could get home to Elizabeth. His preoccupation with seeing her ultimately clouded his judgment. When the 7th Cavalry was within seventy-five miles of Fort Sedgwick, George decided to change course and make for Fort Wallace in western Kansas, which wasn't that far from Fort Hays, where Elizabeth was staying. Just before the troops arrived at the post, George sent couriers out with messages; one was for the commander at Fort Sedgwick, asking for further orders, and the second was for his wife. George wanted her to join him. "If you get a chance to come to Wallace, I will send a squadron there to meet you," George urged Elizabeth. "I am on a roving commission, going nowhere in particular."[38]

The courier delivered the message to Elizabeth, but there was no time to respond. Heavy rains in the area and sudden flooding forced her and the civilians with her to travel to higher ground at Fort Riley.[39]

Two weeks passed with no word from Elizabeth. An anonymous letter about Elizabeth did reach George, however. The correspondence warned George that he should "look after his wife more closely,"[40] and suggested that she was emotionally attached to another man. Immediately following the shocking accusation came news that cholera had broken out at Fort Leavenworth and spread west to Fort Riley. Many people had died from the disease, and George was frantic to know if his wife was among them. Rather than carry on with his superior's orders, which were to "continue after the Cheyenne, using Fort Wallace for a base," George decided to deviate from them and begged leave to visit Elizabeth.[41]

On July 19, 1867, Elizabeth sat alone in her quarters at Fort Riley. Her eyes were bleary from crying over the lack of letters from George. None of the usual activities with which she regularly amused herself—sewing, reading, painting— held her interest. Her despair ended when George suddenly arrived. "The door behind which I paced uneasily, opened, and with a flood of sunshine that poured in, came a vision far brighter than even the brilliant Kansas sun," Elizabeth recalled in her memoirs. "There before me, blithe and buoyant, stood my husband! In an instant, every moment of the preceding moment was obliterated."[42]

George would pay for his mad dash to see his wife. A discontented captain in his charge and the colonel who had granted him leave from duty leveled charges against him. The colonel told authorities that he was not fully awake when George had asked him if he could travel to Fort Riley, and denied giving him permission. The captain told military officials that George was excessively cruel to the men in his command, citing George's order to shoot deserters as an example.

"I knew my orders," George admitted to the army's disciplinary board. "But I made my own decision and acted on it. I think I was right, and I'd do the same thing again if I had to. I'll answer for what I did before the court and take the consequences, whatever they are."[43]

The court-martial proceedings began in August 1867. Elizabeth, along with a number of George's friends and comrades in arms, considered them to be "nothing but an outbreak of the smoldering enmity and envy" often expressed toward her husband. Among the men who testified on George's behalf and praised him for his courage and leadership ability were Tom Custer and Thomas Weir. Thomas sat close beside Elizabeth during the trial. She sat at rigid attention throughout most of the unpleasant event, although at times, while listening to the harsh criticism of her husband, she seemed to weaken. Thomas would gently drape his arm around Elizabeth's shoulders and comfort her. George's eye seldom left the review board; his posture was straight as a steel ramrod.[44]

Benteen watched the scene unfold from the back row of the courtroom. He still believed George to be an "over-confident braggart," and felt that he had failed to make a "meaningful effort" to handle the recent events according to military regulations. Benteen and several other members of the cavalry anticipated that the judge in the trial would find George guilty and that his army career would be over. From Benteen's perspective, more than George's career was in jeopardy. He observed the interaction between Elizabeth and Thomas. It appeared that Thomas couldn't keep his eyes off her, and Elizabeth seemed to relish the attention. George seemed wholly unaware of the connection between the two, his face set determinedly on the courtroom proceedings.[45]

CHAPTER SIX

CUSTER'S MAIDEN

*Girls needn't try to get her dear Bo away from her,
because he loves only her, and her always.*

—GEORGE CUSTER TO ELIZABETH CUSTER, 1871

The day was gray, and a raw, cold wind swirled outside the
windows of the late judge Daniel Bacon's home in Monroe, Michigan. It was early fall, 1868. The judge's daughter,
Elizabeth, and son-in-law, George, sat inside the parlor of
the stately home, each quietly involved in his or her own
task. George was hunched over a writing table, working
on a book about his days at West Point. Elizabeth set aside
some sewing she was doing and drifted over to a piano in
the corner of the room. Her husband glanced up from his
writing long enough to see that Elizabeth wasn't going far.
After weeks of being apart, he wanted her near him at all
times.[1]

The genteel army wife made herself comfortable at the
polished keyboard and then reached for a stack of music
bound in a faded leather pouch. She untied the ribbon holding the music together and sifted through the pages. Inside
one of the pieces of sheet music was a daguerreotype of

George. It had been taken in April 1865, and he was dressed in the uniform of a major general, the two stars on his collar clearly displayed. Some of the music had left its imprint on the picture, the notes like a melody over his face. Elizabeth sat her husband's picture on the stand next to the song she selected and began to play. The ebullient sound filled the air. Although he was tapping his foot in time with the beat, George's attention was trained on the assignment before him.

For a moment Elizabeth wondered if he might only be pretending to be engrossed in writing. She worried that he longed to be doing something else. Nearly a year had passed since a nine-member military jury had found George guilty of "leaving his post without permission, excessive cruelty, and illegal conduct in putting down mutiny in the 7th Cavalry by shooting deserters." The punishment he had received as a result of the court-martial was a year's suspension from rank, duty, and pay.[2]

Courts-martial were commonplace at the time. More than half the army servicemen were court-martialed in 1867 alone. Far from feeling disgraced by the ordeal, the Custers planned to spend the time away from the job and the frontier enjoying one another's company, entertaining family, and traveling abroad.[3] After a short respite from frontline service, however, Elizabeth began to doubt how long George would remain content away from active duty. She knew how much her husband loved the soldier's life. He had once admitted, "I would be willing, yes glad, to see a battle every day during my life."[4]

Prior to the court-martial, while George was either engaged in fights with the Plains Indians or in pursuit of tribes who would not willingly relocate to reservations, Elizabeth hadn't been far from her husband's side. In fact, this is where she had been since he'd been appointed lieutenant colonel of the United States 7th Cavalry Regiment in 1866, and they had traveled to Fort Riley. On the rare occasions when they had been separated because George was happily in battle or celebrating a victory, their marriage had suffered.[5]

Adjutant Captain Thomas Weir had acted as Elizabeth's protector during George's absence in June 1867. Custer had led his troops to Fort McPherson, Nebraska, leaving his wife 215 miles behind, with Thomas and several other members of the 7th Cavalry. Thomas had escorted her on walks and rides outside of Fort Hays and had helped her to safety when flooding threatened to overtake the post and surrounding areas.[6] Rumor had it that Thomas was in love with Elizabeth, but he admired General Custer too much to fully act on his feelings. Elizabeth relished the attention Thomas paid to her but would not consider betraying her husband.[7]

George's mad dash across miles of plains to get to Elizabeth when he thought she might have been stricken with cholera was viewed by his wife as romantic. Whatever pull Thomas Weir had on Elizabeth's affections faded, at least to some extent, after George's grand gesture. The Custers arrived on the other side of the court-martial closer than ever. From Fort Harker, Kansas, where George remained until the hearing, to Fort Leavenworth, Kansas, where they were transferred after the ordeal, the pair was seldom apart.[8]

Elizabeth and George's time on the inactive duty roster was filled with trips back and forth to Monroe, where they attended various social functions. While at the army post they hosted dinner parties and picnics for the officers who had once served under George. Elizabeth took long walks along the river with her cousin Rebecca, who visited from Michigan. They also went to the theater regularly. George tended to the numerous dogs he owned, went on hunting and fishing trips, and attended mule races. But the flurry of events did not keep George from thinking about being back with his troops. He read newspaper accounts of the 7th Cavalry's accomplishments, and speculated on what military leaders would have them do next to contend with the frustrated Indians.[9]

"General Sheridan is in control now," George told Elizabeth in September 1868. "The Cheyenne are on the warpath again, and Sheridan sent the 7th out after them under General Sully. The troops took quite a beating. And the 7th's the best regiment on the plains!"[10]

General Alfred Sully was the commander of the cavalry troops dispatched to deal with the renegade Indians who had killed 124 settlers in a sixty-day period. Head of the Department of the Missouri, General Philip Sheridan, ordered Sully to attack and kill the Indians. "The more we kill," he reasoned, "the less will have to be killed the next year. For the more I see of these Indians, the more I am convinced that they will all have to be killed or maintained as a species of paupers."[11]

The 7th Cavalry did indeed come up against the warring Plains tribes, and the army did not fare well. Cheyenne leader Chief Roman Nose and his braves consistently resisted the cavalry's attempts to subdue them. In early September 1868, fifty of the chief's warriors attacked a detachment of troops in the vicinity of Fort Dodge. Reinforcements arrived and drove the attackers back, but not before the cavalry had sustained several casualties.[12]

George lamented the fact that he wasn't there to help the men who had once been his comrades in arms. Elizabeth comforted her husband as best she could, but knew nothing short of him rejoining his regiment would satisfy him. At almost the same time Elizabeth was worrying about how to help George, General Sheridan realized how much he needed Custer's military expertise and sheer nerve. He sent a letter to U.S. military leaders in Washington, D.C., asking that George be restored to duty.[13] Sheridan sent another wire to George before hearing from his superiors. "General Sherman, Sully, and myself, and nearly all the officers of your regiment, have asked for you, and I hope the application will be successful. Can you come at once?"[14]

George did not wait for a reply from Washington. After answering Sheridan's telegram and assuring him that he was eager to report to work and would soon be on his way, he began packing.

"May I go with you?" Elizabeth asked him.

He shook his head. "Not on this trip," he told her, patting her shoulder. "There won't be time for you to get ready. You understand, don't you, Libbie?"

"Yes," Elizabeth answered, managing a smile. She understood all too well. George was headed into danger.[15]

While en route to Fort Hays, where George was to meet Sheridan, he reread an article from the *Monroe Commercial Newspaper,* headlined THE INDIAN OUTRAGES IN KANSAS. The article began: "Dispatches from General Sheridan confirm the press dispatches about further Indian outrages. General Sheridan says the outrages are too horrible to detail. . . . He is ordered to continue the pursuit and drive the savages from that section of the country, and when captured, to give them summary punishment."[16]

General Sheridan wanted George to take eleven companies, a total of eight hundred men, and drive out the Indians camping along Medicine Lodge Creek in south Kansas, northeast of the Wichita Mountains in Indian Territory (now Oklahoma).[17] The plan was to "engage the entire enemy population." George and his troops were to chase the Arapaho, Kiowa, Comanche, and Cheyenne out of their dwellings and destroy their ponies, food, and all of their belongings. Any women and children killed in this "total war" tactic were to be considered collateral damage.[18]

George arrived at his company's headquarters in early October and quickly set about organizing his men for the winter campaign. On October 4, 1868, he wrote to Elizabeth to let her know where he was and how things were going. "I breakfasted with General Sheridan and staff," he informed her. He told her that the general was pleased to see him, reporting that Sheridan had said: "Custer, I rely on you for everything, and shall send you on this expedition without orders, leaving you to act entirely on your own judgment." Elizabeth knew that this was exactly the type of assignment George had hoped to be given.[19]

For more than a month George and Elizabeth were able to easily exchange letters with one another. Elizabeth kept George abreast of life at Fort Leavenworth and her travels back to Michigan, and George updated his wife on the preparations being made for the coming battles. On November 7, 1868, George wrote to Elizabeth about an unexpected camp visitor: "It is a white woman . . . and she can give me no account of herself," he noted. "She has been four days without food. Our cook is now giving her something to eat. I can only explain her coming by supposing her to have been captured by the Indians, and their barbarous treatment having rendered her insane."[20] George sent the woman to Fort Dodge with the mail party. Her tragic condition made him anxious for the fighting to commence.

As the winter months progressed, George led the 7th Cavalry deep into Indian Territory. Sleet and snow made travel difficult, and it was nearly impossible to find the trail of the Indians, who seemed not to be aware of their presence.[21]

No matter how intolerable the weather or how treacherous the journey, George was dedicated to maintaining his correspondence with his wife. In addition to sharing the details of their expedition, he wrote about the various conversations he had with his staff members and friends, and the animosity Captain Benteen continued to harbor toward him during this assignment. He also wrote to Elizabeth about his plans for their future and how a few of the couples they knew had been affected by the devastating impact of separation.

George's letter made Elizabeth suspicious. She read and reread George's account of a marriage that was struggling as a result of the length of time the two had been separated. A mutual acquaintance of theirs had succumbed to alcohol after becoming convinced his wife had been unfaithful while they were away from one another. "She is with him, but he scarcely notices her now," George wrote to Elizabeth, ". . . and from the excellent officer that he once was, he has descended to one of the most inefficient. Poor man, I am deeply sorry for him and cannot censure him. I would do no better if as well were I in his place. . . . How blessed am I that I am united to a pure, virtuous and devoted wife, and I feel immeasurably thankful for it."[22]

In their letters to one another, the Custers had often discussed their desire to have children. They both wanted to add to their family, but had not been blessed with off-spring.* George suggested that he and Elizabeth adopt his ten-year-old nephew, Henry Armstrong Reed, also known

---

* Historians have speculated that both George and Elizabeth may have had health issues that kept them from having children. One theory is that George was sterile as a result of the trauma of hard riding—an occupational hazard in the cavalry. It has also been speculated that George may have contracted gonorrhea prior to his marriage, which could have caused sterility as well. (Utley, Robert M., *Cavalier in Buckskin: George Armstrong Custer and the Western Military Frontier*, p. 193; Welsh, Jack D., *Medical Histories of Union Generals*, p. 88.)

as Armstrong. Henry was the son of George's sister Lydia, but was particularly close to his aunt Elizabeth and uncle George. Elizabeth considered the proposal but ultimately decided against it.[23]

Letters between George and Elizabeth came to a temporary halt on November 22, 1868, after George received orders from General Sheridan to take his men to the Washita River. Through a thick, fast-falling snow, a scout had come across the trail of a war party, 150 men strong. Wearing buffalo shoes and fur caps with ear lappets, the cavalry marched toward the unsuspecting Indian encampment. No one spoke as they moved forward to a position a few miles from their objective. George did not want to give away the 7th Cavalry's position, so the horses were halted for fear their hooves might be heard crunching in the snow. He requested that the soldiers remove their sabers from their belts to prevent them from clanking, and communications were reduced to hand signals. The troops waited in eerie silence for the moment they would make their move.[24]

The sound of the cavalry's imminent attack resonated throughout the frigid area at the break of dawn. More than eight hundred soldiers charged the sleeping camp. George yelled out orders at the troops. The attack was swift and the suffering intense. Many men, women, and children were killed. An oozing layer of bodies covered the ground afterward. George referred to the scene as "unutterable carnage." Two Kiowa Indian leaders were taken captive, along with several Apache chiefs and braves, and 875 ponies were rounded up. George selected the best animals out of the herd for the regiment and had the remaining horses shot and killed.[25]

Troops searched the tepees, looking for survivors and seizing property that included pictures, fragments of letters, bits of bedding, clothing from slain Kansas homesteaders, and military documents taken from unfortunate dispatchers. George was eager to report to his commanding officers with news of the discovery, the outcome of the battle, and the officers who had displayed "patience and gallantry." Frederick Benteen was one of the men he complimented for his daring.[26]

In addition to braves and chiefs, the soldiers took a number of women and children captive. George asked his interpreter, Romeo, to gather all the prisoners together in one area so he could assure them they would be treated kindly, and to let them know what was expected of them in return.[27] Once they were assembled, George scanned the faces of the frightened Indians, and, in a calm but authoritative voice, addressed the captives. At the conclusion of his talk, one of the older Cheyenne women stepped forward, leading a young girl by the hand. After introducing the teenager to George and his troops as Monahsetah, the woman placed the young girl's hand in Custer's and proceeded to deliver what seemed to be a benediction in Cheyenne. A few curious moments passed before George turned to the interpreter and asked, "What is this woman doing?" Romeo explained with a grin that the squaw was marrying him and Monahsetah.[28]

Bewildered, yet somewhat amused, George quickly dropped the young girl's hand. He had no intention of becoming her husband. He expressed his appreciation for the act of kindness and politely excused himself. "After the battle the old squaws were as full of admiration for the successful troopers as they were for their liege lords," George wrote to Elizabeth, weeks after the event. "Their willingness to part with their daughters was quite equal to that of the predatory mother in the States, who is accused of roaming from one watering-place to another in search of game."[29]

Monahsetah was seventeen years old when she met George, and seven months pregnant. Estranged from her husband, Brown Bear, the tall beauty was highly sought after by other braves in her tribe. According to her great-great-granddaughter, Gail Kelly-Custer, "Monahsetah was told by her elders that her destiny lay with a man who would come from the stars." When she first saw George, she believed the prophecy had come true. "He was on a magnificent horse, wearing Indian buckskins, but with a bright red sash tied at his throat and waving a long, shiny knife," Monahsetah later shared with family. "He was magnificent as well, and was in front, leading the Blue Coats, yelling with a deep, resonating voice, 'Come on, boys!' His hair was long and wavy, flowing in the wind as if like fire, the color of Cheyenne red. It seemed to glow on its own."[30]

Shortly after the battle at Washita, the 7th Cavalry responded to orders to return to Camp Supply, Oklahoma, a U.S. Army post established in Indian Territory to protect the Southern Plains, with their captives. Monahsetah acted as a scout and a goodwill representative between George and the hostile Indians with the caravan. She also served as an additional interpreter. She spoke to the Plains Indians using sign language and taught George the signs that he was lacking. She also proved to be an expert tracker. She was able to examine the bones, fur, and skin of the game killed by the Indian parties that had set up camp in the area. The condition of the marrow in the bones told her how much time had passed since the game had been killed, and that information could be translated into how far away the tribe might be.[31]

George was grateful to Monahsetah for her cooperation and also somewhat infatuated with her. In his autobiography he described her as "an exceedingly comely squaw, possessing a bright, cheery face, a countenance beaming with intelligence, and a disposition more inclined to be merry than one usually finds among Indians. . . . Added to the bright, laughing eyes, a set of pearly teeth, and a rich complexion, her well-shaped head was crowned with a luxuriant growth of the most beautiful silken tresses . . ."[32]

When the 7th Cavalry marched triumphantly into Camp Supply, Monahsetah rode at George's side while the other captives rode behind the scouts. Once the camp officers had reviewed the troops, the Indians were escorted to their temporary quarters, and with the exception of Monahsetah, kept under guard. She was allowed to roam the post undisturbed by the soldiers, and in the days that followed, she was often seen in George's company.[33]

Captain Benteen kept a watchful eye on Monahsetah and the man she called "Son of the Morning Star." He claimed that George allowed his closest friends to "take their pick" of the Indian women being held and that George himself was "consorting with the comely woman called Monahsetah." Benteen vowed to make sure that Elizabeth was made aware of Monahsetah and the relationship she had with George.[34]

George wrote to Elizabeth about the Indian woman, sharing with her the valuable service Monahsetah had offered during their attempts to bring about the tribe's surrender. George explained what had happened in a series of letters to Elizabeth: "When couriers from among the Indians, who had previously given themselves up, had been sent out to their village to try to induce the others to come in, Monahsetah had been consulted and her advise [sic] taken." Monahsetah was unable to reason with all of the Indians she helped to locate; those steadfast few refused to be moved off their ancestral land.[35]

Less than a week after arriving at Camp Supply, the 7th Cavalry, along with twelve companies of the 19th Kansas Volunteer Cavalry, set out to round up hostile Kiowa, Cheyenne, and Arapaho Indians who chose not to surrender and move to the reservation. Some had fled into the wilderness, while others went north to join the Sioux renegades. Accompanying the column, at George's request, was Monahsetah. He maintained that her presence was necessary because she knew the terrain.[36]

On December 8, 1868, George wrote a quick letter to Elizabeth to let her know that the 7th Cavalry was at Fort Cobb (in what is now Oklahoma) and that the post would be their winter headquarters. "Here we are after 12 days' marching," he wrote to his wife, "through snow and an almost impassable country where sometimes we made only eight miles a day, following an Indian trail. . . ."[37] George and his troops were kept busy in the days that followed, subduing warring tribes and forcing them onto reservations.

In mid-January 1869, Monahsetah gave birth to a son. Women at the fort who were ignorant of the length of time George had known her believed the baby was his, and were quick to spread that rumor. George wrote to Elizabeth about Monahsetah's baby boy and how enamored most of the people at the fort were with the child.[38]

When George led his troops on an expedition to capture Indians who had not lived up to the agreement to surrender themselves to the army, and rescue two white women who had been kidnapped, Monahsetah and her son rode with them. The first day out she was able to help locate the trail of the Cheyenne Indians who were holding the women hostage, but the tracks were old. For sixteen days the cavalry searched for fresh tracks. Each time they located new tracks, the prints would quickly be lost in the falling snow.[39]

The expedition proved to be long and grueling. Supplies were eventually depleted, and soldiers and dependents were forced to live on mule meat. George navigated his beleaguered command to Fort Sill, Oklahoma. After his troops got a few days of rest and plenty to eat, George made plans to continue the journey. The next venture out was successful. Monahsetah and the other scouts located the Cheyenne village, and George and his men quickly encircled the Indian camp. He held his troops back rather than attack because he feared the first shot fired would be the signal for killing the white prisoners.[40]

When the Indians discovered they were surrounded, they decided to invite George to meet with their chiefs. George agreed to the risky proposition, but mapped out a plan to deal with the potential danger he knew could arise. Led by the tribe medicine man, the Indians first participated in a ceremony of prayers and chanting designed to strike their enemies down.[41] Next, the chiefs brought in entertainers and attempted to create a distraction so their people could slip away with the white captives. George then put his plan into action. He had his troops apprehend the chiefs and then offered to trade the men for the white women. The Indians refused. Per orders issued by General Sheridan, George started to hang the chiefs. At that point the women were released and the Cheyenne surrendered.[42]

George, Monahsetah, and the others returned to Camp Supply at the conclusion of the expedition. Rather than escort the Cheyenne to the reservation, George was ordered to leave them at the post with the other Indians captured at the Battle of Washita. He was instructed to continue to Fort Hays. During the five-day journey from post to post, George and Monahsetah spent a great deal of time together. Rumor had it that Monahsetah was visiting the general's tent at night.[43]

Elizabeth received an anonymous letter informing her that George had been unfaithful.[44] She quickly made arrangements to travel to Fort Hays and was waiting there when George and Monahsetah arrived. After embracing her husband and congratulating him on the job he did, Elizabeth turned her attention to Monahsetah. She was less impressed with the Indian maiden's appearance than George had been. "Her face was not pretty in repose, except with the beauty of youth, whose dimples and curves and rounded outlines are always charming," she recalled in her memoirs.[45]

As the two women stood eyeing one another, Elizabeth noted that she felt a bit nervous. "How could I help feeling that when with a swift movement she would produce a hidden weapon," she later wrote, "and by stabbing the wife, hurt the white chief who had captured her, in what she believed would be the most cruel way."

Elizabeth's fears were put to rest when Monahsetah presented her baby to her. "It was a cunning little bundle of brown velvet," she remembered, "with the same bright, bead-like eyes as the rest . . . She [Monahsetah] was full of maternal pride."[46]

Six months after George and Monahsetah had first met, the Indian woman left with the other Indian captives to live on the Cheyenne reservation. "Monahsetah walked out of the [post] gate, her papoose on her back, smiling and shy, and showing some regret at departure," Elizabeth remembered.[47]

In the autumn of 1870, Monahsetah gave birth to another son. The infant was a flaxen-haired, light-skinned boy she named Yellow Swallow. Indian legend has it that the child's father was George Custer.[48]

Elizabeth knew Monahsetah possessed a strong sense of loyalty to George and recognized that her husband was grateful for the maiden's devotion, but she was certain that their marriage could endure. George's critics, such as Benteen, found it easy to believe he had fathered a child with Monahsetah, but Elizabeth disregarded the notion.

Those close to the Custers suggested that George's thoughts of Monahsetah did not fade as quickly as Elizabeth would have liked and that she resented the Indian woman.[49] They tried to overcome their emotional estrangement by reacquainting themselves with one another at Fort Hays.

The post had changed substantially since the floodwaters had overtaken it in 1867. Rows of small, newly constructed homes lined the main thoroughfare of the camp, and new trees had been planted in between the buildings.[50] Although army officers were offered private living quarters, the Custers declined the government housing, choosing instead to live in canvas tents. The entire 7th Cavalry was encamped in tents near a creek not far from Fort Hays. George wanted to be near his men, and Elizabeth wanted to be near her husband.

Elizabeth was very happy with their home, cobbled together from assorted tents requisitioned from the regimental quartermaster for the summer. "We felt very rich," she recalled in her autobiography, "for by borrowing from our Uncle Sam, we had as many rooms as some houses have. . . ." There was a parlor, bedroom, and a kitchen. A carpenter built a deck at the rear entrance of the caravan of tents. George and Elizabeth spent a great deal of time on their deck. He read and she sewed. "We imagined the creek to be the Hudson, and the cotton-wood, whose foliage is anything but thick, to be a graceful maple or stately, branching elm," Elizabeth remembered.[51]

The massacre at the Battle of Washita halted attacks by renegade Plains Indians, and with the exception of the occasional buffalo-hunting expedition and some horse-racing events, the cavalry was mostly inactive. Routine patrol trips held no interest. George was bored. In June 1869, he applied for a command position at West Point. His application was quickly denied. The army valued George's presence on the volatile frontier too much.[52]

The Custers made several trips to the town of Hays, Kansas, to stop and visit with Bill Hickok. George and Elizabeth had met Hickok in 1867 while he was serving as a scout for the army. He became sheriff of Hays in 1869. Elizabeth found Hickok to be "strikingly handsome." She wrote, "Physically, he was a delight to look upon. Tall, lithe and free in every motion. He rode and walked as if every muscle was perfection. . . ." Elizabeth would have been content living on the vast trackless plains with her husband and traveling to see Bill Hickok, but George needed more.[53]

Before the first heavy snowfall covered the prairie, Elizabeth, George, and his troops were en route to Fort Leavenworth. After he arrived, he asked his superior officers for a short leave of absence to take care of family business in Monroe. He also wanted to visit his friends in New York and to look in on an ailing General Philip Sheridan in Chicago Elizabeth reluctantly stayed behind in Fort Leavenworth.[54]

Benteen speculated in his autobiography that George's departure was in part prompted by the strain in his marriage brought on by alliances with Monahsetah and other "peccadilloes." Benteen insisted that Elizabeth was aware of George's roaming eye, but chose to overlook it because she didn't want to sacrifice the fame associated with being his wife. "Mrs. Custer is just about as avaricious and parsimonious a woman as you can find in a day's walk," he wrote to a friend in 1897.[55]

George and Elizabeth were separated off and on for several months. Their relationship would be subjected to more gossip and innuendo before they were reunited.

CHAPTER SEVEN

TROUBLE APART

*I would be willing, yes, glad, to see a battle every day
during my life.*

—GEORGE CUSTER, OCTOBER 1862

Spirited music and laughter burst through the doors of
Chicago's Opera House. The velveteen drapes subdued the
whir of roulette wheels that lined the theater lobby and
muffled the voices of the faro dealers. Patrons poured into
the establishment, seeking entertainment and shelter from
the freezing cold. Chicago was a city of handsome dwellings
whose elegance and refinements were reflected in the brilliant social life. A throb beat through its every artery. One
of the many acts that attracted the attention of the bustling
crowds was Lydia Thompson's British Blondes. This troupe
of celebrated actresses, boasting overwhelming propor-
tions and specializing in dancing and pantomime, performed nightly for packed houses. They had many devoted
famous fans, including the Grand Duke Alexis of Russia,
Wild Bill Hickok, and George Custer.[1]

Over the Thanksgiving holiday in 1869, when George
had left for his travels east without Elizabeth, he had

attended the show a couple of times, enjoying not only the burlesque styling of the irresistible sirens, but also partaking in the popular games of chance that greeted people when they entered the building. George had been in Michigan taking care of family business and then he had traveled to Illinois to visit Philip Sheridan, his former army commander and respected mentor, who was ill.[2] News that he was in the Windy City spread quickly, and George was soon inundated with invitations to attend dinners and theatrical openings. His reputation as a soldier and military leader, along with the numerous articles he had written about his combat experience, preceded him.[3] Everyone wanted to be in George's company, and he delighted in the attention.

Local newspapers reported on his outings, giving special concentration to the fact that Elizabeth was not at his side. "George Custer," one article began, "has been seen about without his wife, chasing blondes instead of Indian maidens."[4] He made light of the report in a letter he wrote to Elizabeth, letting her know that in addition to the British Blondes show, he had also taken in a play featuring the best-known comedian of the day, Joseph Jefferson. "I never had so nice a time in all my life—expect when I am with you," George assured his wife.[5]

Elizabeth read over her husband's letters from their quarters at Fort Leavenworth, Kansas. She usually accompanied George in his travels, but for this trip she had decided to remain behind. Her cousin, Anne Bingham, was coming to visit, and she hadn't wanted to miss spending time with her. After receiving George's letter Elizabeth wished she had gone with him. Along with the list of entertaining activities, his correspondence contained some worrisome information about playing cards with friends. George was a gambler who found it difficult to resist a game.[6]

The Custers' marriage had been strained since George's involvement with the Cheyenne woman, Monahsetah. Elizabeth had tolerated their friendship and had tried to dismiss talk from the Cheyenne that the maiden and George were husband and wife. George assured Elizabeth that this assumption was based on cultural misunderstanding. His compulsive gambling could not be explained away so easily, however.[7] The sometimes-expensive habit had added to problems in their relationship. On January 1, 1870, George would make a solemn vow to reform, pledging to cease from "playing cards or any other game of chance for money or its equivalent." He had not made any similar promises with regard to women.[8]

Elizabeth lamented the distance, both physical and emotional, between herself and George. The barrage of company she had daily was a welcome distraction. Fort Leavenworth was a forward destination for thousands of soldiers, surveyors, immigrants, Indians, preachers, and settlers passing through, and it was not unusual for many of these individuals to drop by the Custer home to pay their respects. Thomas Weir was a regular visitor. He took it upon himself to make sure Elizabeth was well cared for while George was away.[9] She was grateful for his concern, but missed her husband. She was taken aback when George decided to extend his leave and visit the East Coast.

George had stopped by the War Department in Philadelphia when he learned that the 7th Cavalry was being divided into two groups. Officials at the War Department were working on getting the 7th Cavalry Regiment away from the Department of Missouri, because a regiment on the Pacific Coast wanted to take its place. If that happened, George wanted to follow the company's headquarters to the post where it would be assigned. Colonel Samuel Sturgis, head of the 7th Cavalry Regiment, wholeheartedly approved of the idea.[10] Elizabeth was disappointed, but tried to appreciate how restless George became when he was without orders to fight or participate in training missions.

George was delayed in Philadelphia, discussing the 7th Cavalry's future, and missed spending Christmas with his wife in 1869. Captain George Yates, a member of Custer's staff, escorted Elizabeth and her cousin, Anne Bingham, to the enlisted men's mess hall to enjoy a traditional turkey dinner. The cousins celebrated the New Year with Yates and the troops as well.[11] By then, George was en route to New York. In his first letter to Elizabeth in 1870, he expressed his displeasure at being away from the frontier. "I feel so cooped up," he noted. "There's nothing like the space and sunlight of the plains. I tell you, Libbie, I'd rather be an ordinary trooper in the cavalry and out there than an important officer in the infantry anywhere else in the country!"[12]

George managed to get past his unhappiness about not being on the frontier by visiting with old friends from West Point and taking in the sights of the city. He was never lacking for company. Bold women who knew of George's accomplishments introduced themselves to him at art exhibits or restaurants. He was forthcoming about his various encounters in his letters to Elizabeth. Oftentimes he would brag to her about the "good-looking young women who spoke with him."[13]

One of the better-known women competing for his notice was opera singer Clara Louise Kellogg. George admired Clara, who was independent, enterprising, a smart businesswoman, and completely indifferent to romance. According to George, their relationship was purely platonic. "I care for no one in town," he admitted to Elizabeth, "but Miss Kellogg. I respect her and she respects me."[14] After George attended one of her performances at the Academy of Music, the soprano invited him to a behind-the-scenes tour of the theater. He described the experience in a letter to his wife as "perfect."[15]

Referring to Elizabeth in a letter as "Darling, Standby," George wrote that he suspected some of the women who sought him out had more on their mind than friendship. They paced back and forth in front of his hotel room, hoping he would see them and offer to accompany them on their way. George felt that sculptor Vinnie Ream wanted more than a platonic relationship. The twenty-one-year-old artist asked George to be present at the unveiling of her statue of President Abraham Lincoln. Fearing he might give her the wrong impression, George declined the invitation.[16]

He was aware that some people felt his association with any woman other than his wife was inappropriate.

They misinterpreted his friendship with Clara and believed he was frequently unfaithful to Elizabeth. "The old Irish servant who takes care of my room looks at me with suspicion when I return, sometimes not till morning, the bed having not been touched," George confided in a letter written to Elizabeth from New York in July 1871. "I think she believes I do not pass my nights in the most reputable manner. In fact, circumstances, as she sees them, are against me."[17]

It wasn't uncommon for George to include information about the seemingly endless parade of young ladies interested in him in his letters to his wife. Elizabeth generally overlooked his attempts to make her jealous. Rumors of a possible romance between Elizabeth and Thomas Weir continued to circulate, however, and George had difficulty dismissing them outright.[18]

It wasn't George's wandering eye that caused the most trouble in the Custers' marriage. George couldn't resist revealing his true feelings for her each time he wrote. "I love you," he reminded Elizabeth. "You and you alone." It was actually the questionable way in which he handled money that gave Elizabeth pause. George speculated on railroad stocks with borrowed money, plunging into ventures he knew nothing about, such as mining.[19]

George was a social success while on leave from the army in early 1871, and he wanted his professional life to be equally as successful. In February 1871, he hoped to supplement his military pay with investments in racehorses and gold and silver mines. He had researched the rumors of rich silver finds in Clear Creek, Colorado, and determined that the potential to make a fortune was viable. His goal was to purchase the eastern half of the Stevens' Lode outside of the community of Georgetown, but for that, he needed capital. He actively pursued financiers and raised more than $35,000, along with personally investing some of his own money in the venture.[20]

Although Elizabeth had doubts about George's get-rich-quick schemes, he was always optimistic. He believed a promising buyer for his shares in the mine would come along and make him a wealthy man. In April 1871, a buyer did arrive and purchased an interest in the project. "Can it be," he wrote to Elizabeth, "that my little standby and I, who have long wished to possess a small fortune, are about to have our hopes and wishes realized?"[21]

When George wasn't working on ways to make money above and beyond his military income, he was seeking relief from the rigors of the business world. He frequented boxing matches and horse races in Buffalo and Saratoga, New York. Although many around him were wagering on the outcome of the events, he kept the promise he had made to Elizabeth to refrain from betting.[22]

George was constantly on the go, and most of the time missed his wife terribly. "How I wish you were here to double my joys and quadruple my expenses in this enchanting place," he wrote to Elizabeth from Saratoga. "I enjoy everything except being away from you." George's tone was a lot more inviting than the correspondence Elizabeth had received earlier that summer. In those letters, he had expressed his displeasure with her about writing to some of the men who used to serve on his staff. He didn't like the idea of Elizabeth wishing any man well but him.[23]

In May 1871, George accused Elizabeth of sharing the letters he had written to her with Myles Keogh, one of the captains in the 7th Cavalry. News of the route George was going to take to get to his post in Kentucky was made known to Keogh. "How did it reach him?" he queried Elizabeth. "If I was of a suspicious disposition I would imagine you had informed him. . . ."[24]

By late August he had set aside his frustrations and apologized for his behavior. He ached to be reunited with his wife. He'd received news from the army that his leave was officially over and that he was to report to Elizabethtown, Kentucky. He quickly sent word to Elizabeth about the orders and made arrangements for her to meet him in Monroe. From there he would escort her to Louisville, and then on to his command. "Personally I should have preferred the Plains . . . ," he wrote to Elizabeth. "Duty in the South has somewhat of a political aspect, which I always seek to avoid."[25]

Members of the 7th Cavalry had been dispatched to the area ahead of George and disseminated throughout the Southern states on a mission to rout out the Ku Klux Klan. Elizabeth was cautiously optimistic about being with George again. She sent a letter to her aunt explaining that he had sold his controlling interest in the mine and was ready to begin a new chapter in their lives—one free from doubts or insinuations.[26]

The Custers were happy to see one another when they met in Michigan, but things between them were a bit strained. They slowly became reacquainted with one another during the two-week trip to the Kentucky post. A stopover in Louisville to shop for horses helped ease the tension. They arrived at the military camp on September 21, 1871. Both were underwhelmed by Elizabethtown. It was an economically depressed area with little to do outside of watching the livestock.[27]

Elizabeth busied herself with decorating their quarters, writing letters home, and sewing. George bought her a sewing machine, and she made clothes for herself, her husband, and brother-in-law. Together the Custers attended dances and enjoyed picnic outings with friends. George's leisure time was spent hunting, writing articles and his war reminiscences, and reading. He shared the stresses of overseeing two companies of the 7th Cavalry and their assignments with Elizabeth.[28]

Whenever possible, Elizabeth traveled with George when he was called away from the post on business. In a letter to a friend written in October 1871, she noted that she gladly went along with him because she was always in need of a respite from the dullness of Elizabethtown. Sometimes Elizabeth ventured off by herself. She would travel to Lexington, Kentucky, and Cincinnati, Ohio, to consult with dressmakers on the latest fashions and fabrics. George was then forced to endure the tour alone, and he didn't care for it. "This is the last leave you get from your headquarters," he teased Elizabeth in a note he wrote to her in the winter of 1872.[29]

Elizabeth didn't like being apart from George for too long. Not only did she miss him, but it was also easier for him to resist the temptation to gamble when they were together. In February 1872, George reneged on his promise to Elizabeth to give up gambling. He lost $10,000 on racehorses in Bluegrass and Frogtown, Kentucky.[30] Vices notwithstanding, Elizabeth considered his every attempt at being morally upright admirable. She noted in a letter to a family member in Monroe that "everyone in Kentucky drank, but George abstained from any alcoholic beverages. When the gentlemen ask him what he will take, George replies, 'A glass of Alderney,' [a non-alcoholic drink] and toasts in that while they take whiskey, brandy, and wine."[31]

George and Elizabeth shared their home with as many as eighty dogs while stationed at the post. They were good company for the couple, who were equally attached to the animals. Several slept in bed with the pair each night. The Custers doted on the animals with the affection reserved for the children they were unable to have.[32]

When George's brother Tom came to visit, George and Elizabeth showered their attention on him. Friends and cohorts knew the three as "the inseparables." They laughed and played practical jokes on one another. Time in Elizabethtown did not seem to drag when Tom was around. George tried to have his brother transferred from Captain Benteen's battalion in Louisville to his command, but Benteen refused the request. George complained to his wife that Benteen "always did the opposite of what he wanted."[33]

In January 1872, George received word from General Philip Sheridan, who had completely recovered from his illness, that the Custers were going to get a break from their mundane life in Elizabethtown. The nineteen-year-old Grand Duke Alexis of Russia was visiting the United States and wanted to experience the sights, sounds, and activities of America's Wild West. He asked the government to organize a buffalo hunt and allow him to participate. General Sheridan was given the assignment, and called upon George to coach the duke in riding and shooting. William Cody, better known as Buffalo Bill, was asked to come along and serve as a guide.[34]

Elizabeth and George met up with the Grand Duke's elaborate caravan of servants and Russian politicians in Louisville. The massive hunting party proceeded from there by train toward Colorado. Elizabeth chose to remain in Kentucky and enjoy the luxury of the Galt Hotel, where she would stay until her husband returned a few weeks later.

The Grand Duke's trip was a success. After having killed three buffalo, he ordered his train to return to Louisville, Kentucky, where he hosted several lavish balls and multicourse dinners. Elizabeth and George dined and danced with foreign dignitaries and American diplomats who attended each event. According to several major publications, including the *New York Herald* and the *Cambridge Jeffersonian*, members of the Russian royalty's staff were quite taken with Elizabeth's grace and beauty.[35]

Elizabeth was impressed with Admiral Poisset, one of the ranking managing members of the ducal party. "The Admiral is all sunshine and sweet simplicity," Elizabeth noted in her journal on February 5, 1872. The mutual regard Admiral Poisset and Elizabeth had for one another was not lost on George. He was proud of his wife and the attention she received. Conversely, Elizabeth wasn't entirely pleased with George. The Grand Duke and George shared a fondness for pretty women, and in particular, the beautiful, blonde entertainer Lydia Thompson. The two enjoyed discussing her many talents and singing the songs she made popular. Elizabeth resented Lydia being the subject of such in-depth conversation.[36]

The Custers traveled with the Grand Duke until his excursion ended in New Orleans in late February. The Russian royal returned to his native country, and George and Elizabeth returned to Kentucky. For the next year the pair made several trips back and forth to Michigan. They attended weddings in Monroe, military ceremonies in Lexington, and a reunion of Civil War veterans in Detroit. No matter how much activity the Custers scheduled to break up the monotony of living in Elizabethtown, however, nothing compared to the life the cavalry couple had experienced on the Great Plains.[37]

After two years of light duty in the rural South, George received orders to organize the members of the 7th Cavalry for an assignment in the Dakotas. He was ecstatic, and Elizabeth was happy for him. She was also worried. The cavalry's assignment was to protect surveyors and builders working for the Northern Pacific Railroad from attacks by Sioux Indians. Due to the volatile nature of the mission, the government resisted giving wives and family members the chance to accompany their husbands into the region. In March 1873, restrictions were eased and officers' wives were given permission to travel with their spouses. Elizabeth was one of the first wives to make the journey.[38]

A cluster of dark clouds caught the sun trying to shine down on a crudely constructed depot in Yankton, Dakota Territory. Elizabeth paced around the trunks and boxes filled with her and George's personal belongings. George and some of the other members of the regiment had ridden out ahead of their dependents to make sure the temporary camp they were heading to was put together quickly and correctly. Snow was in the forecast, and the travelers needed a dry place to stay for the evening. Once the tents were pitched, George hurried back to the depot to collect his wife.[39]

By the time they made it to the camp, a blizzard had overtaken the area. The drastic change in weather from balmy Kentucky to the frigid Dakotas made some of the cavalrymen ill, and George was not immune. The longer he worked in the wintry climate, the worse he felt. At the end of his daily duties he dragged himself to his tent, exhausted and covered in melting snow.[40]

Although he tried to hide it, Elizabeth quickly realized George was not well. His complexion was extremely pale and he was listless. He needed to be somewhere much warmer and dryer than a tent. While en route to the campsite, Elizabeth had spotted a half-finished cabin among a cluster of barren trees. She decided that George needed to be moved to the cabin. Some of the soldiers helped Elizabeth transport George to the building. A surgeon was called for, and once George was made comfortable, Elizabeth gave him the strong medicine he was prescribed. Using a small cooking stove and wood to warm the cabin, Elizabeth and the Custers' cook, Mary, stripped George of his wet clothing and dressed him in dry garments. The pair covered him with blankets and shawls and fed him broth. His fever skyrocketed as the blizzard howled outside the primitive structure. "The snow was so fine that it penetrated the smallest cracks," Elizabeth recalled in her memoirs, ". . . and soon we found white lines appearing all around us—where the roof joined the walls, on the windows, and under the doors. Outside the air was so thick with the whirling, tiny particles that it was almost impossible to see one's hand held out before one."[41]

The snow continued to fall as Elizabeth nursed George back to health. "The wind shook the loose window casings and sometimes broke in the door," she later noted. The Custers were holed up in the cold cabin for more than fifty-two hours before George's fever broke and he began showing signs of recovery.[42]

George was grateful for his wife's devotion and came to her aid when she was suddenly overcome with the gravity of the situation—the frigid temperatures, combined with his potentially life-threatening illness. Burying her face in her shawl, she sobbed. He comforted her with tender words, and each realized that no matter what problems had occurred in their past, their relationship could and would withstand any obstacle—even death.[43]

CHAPTER EIGHT

Plains Living

My husband used to tell me that he believed he was the happiest man on earth, and I cannot help but thinking he was.

—Elizabeth Custer, 1882

A group of some forty officers and their wives congregated in the parlor of George and Elizabeth Custer's home at Fort Abraham Lincoln in Dakota Territory. A fiddler entertained several men and women at one end of the tastefully decorated room. More guests paraded past a table filled with a variety of food and drinks at the other. Elizabeth remained by the door, kindly welcoming latecomers to the party, already in progress. She touched a finger to her lips, indicating that the attendees should enter quietly.

The music stopped, and a hush fell over the guests. Elizabeth's sister-in-law Margaret Calhoun and her husband, Tom, and family friend Agnes marched into the parlor and crossed to the musicians. All three wore costumes: Maggie was dressed as a Sioux Indian maiden. Agnes and Tom were dressed as Quakers. George and the others in attendance stifled a chuckle as the trio struck a dignified pose for the captive audience. They were acting out a scene from a current event in the region. The object of the entertaining charade, or tableau, was to guess the event and whom the players represented.[1]

Partygoers enthusiastically shouted out their best guesses. Others issued comical remarks that made everyone erupt into laughter. When guests announced that the performers were portraying Quaker missionaries evangelizing Native Americans, the actors broke character and took a bow. The happy audience applauded their efforts, and the music started up again.

Outside it was snowing. A few enlisted men were on guard duty. Wearing layers of scarves and bundled in heavy coats, they romped through the snow past the Custers' house. Horses and wagons filled the yard and were tied to hitching posts below the massive porch in front of the house. Looking in through the windows, the troops could see cheerful, fashionably dressed people enjoying a lively square dance, and they could hear the fiddler playing. The soldiers lingered for a moment, enjoying the view, then continued on their way.

Thirty miles away, on the west bank of the Missouri River at Fort Rice, Frederick Benteen stood outside his barracks staring over the vast plains toward Fort Lincoln. He could almost see his nemesis, George Custer, surrounded by the usual group of followers and celebrating the long winter days with wine and song. He disapproved of George, his wife, and the "clique" that aligned themselves with the couple. Benteen complained that their "conduct

[was] unbecoming an officer, the wife of an officer, and his staff."[2]

Benteen might have felt differently had he been in command of loyal soldiers at a popular camp. Some visitors to the military camp referred to Fort Rice as "one of the most godforsaken spots on the Earth."[3] In comparison to the lonely, near-desolate Fort Rice, Fort Lincoln was Shangri-la.

Five months prior to the Custers being transferred to Fort Lincoln, Benteen, George, and Elizabeth had lived at Fort Rice with the other soldiers, wives, and dependents of the 7th Cavalry. General David Sloane Stanley was the commander of the post, and he had originally disliked George almost as much as Benteen did. For his part, George believed his problems with Stanley could have serious repercussions, and he feared he would end up living out his military career at the army's most-neglected post. George's leadership skills, however, ultimately won over his commanding officer.[4]

The Custers' journey to the Dakota Territory, where George reported to General Stanley for duty, began in Memphis, Tennessee, in late March 1873. All went well until they reached the Dakota Territory, where a massive snowstorm had overcome the party on April 13, and George had become severely ill. Once George was on his feet again, the Custers, along with the other members of the 7th Cavalry, continued on to a post near Yankton, in what is now South Dakota. They were treated well by the locals in the area and were honored guests at several social events.[5]

Shortly after a routine was established at the camp,
George began readying the troops for the 500-mile trek from
Yankton to Fort Rice. Elizabeth was one of only two officers'
wives allowed to join their husbands on the overland journey. The other women (cooks, laundresses, prostitutes)
had to follow the cavalry via steamer down the Yellowstone River. From atop her horse, Polly, Elizabeth watched
the distinguished soldiers and their support vehicles ride
across the countryside. "We never tired of seeing the command advancing," Elizabeth wrote in her memoirs, "with
the long line of supply wagons, under their covers, wind-
ing around bends in the road and climbing over the hills."
She was equally moved by the efficiency of making camp
each evening. When the cavalry arrived at an appropriate
spot to camp for the night, the troops went straight to work,
unloading the wagons, tending to the horses, and preparing
the meals. "An ineffaceable picture remains with me even
now," Elizabeth recalled in her memoir, *Boots and Saddles*.
"The general and I used to think there was no bit of color
equal to the delicate blue lines of smoke which rose from the
campfire, where the soldier's supper was being cooked."[6]

Travel was slow, barely four miles an hour, but the mea-
sured journey gave the Custers a chance to enjoy the lush
region. They found time to go off by themselves and ride
among the cottonwoods that lined the riverbanks. They
encountered Sioux Indian burial grounds, a variety of wildlife, torrential rainfall, and small tornadoes. No matter
what the next horizon revealed, George and Elizabeth cher-
ished every moment of their time together on the trip.[7]

NOTICE.

Whereas, my wife, Mrs. E. Custer leaving left my bed and board without just cause or provocation, all persons are hereby forbidden harboring or trusting her on my account, as I shall pay no debts of her contracting.

Bismarck, D. T., Nov.

CUSTER

George cut and pasted when he was upset with Elizabeth, circa 1875.
Courtesy of Elizabeth Custer Library and Museum at Garryowen, Montana

Elizabeth Bacon Custer
Courtesy of Denver Public Library Western History Collection B-942

The Custers: George Armstrong Custer, his wife, Elizabeth Bacon Custer, and his younger brother, Second Lt. Tom Custer. *Courtesy of Denver Public Library Western History Collection Z-2439*

Brigadier General George Custer
at his headquarters in the field,
Army of the Potomac, Virginia
*Courtesy of Elizabeth Custer Library and
Museum at Garryowen, Montana*

Custer's staff at Austin, Texas,
1865. George Custer sits on the
steps, right of doorway next to
his wife, Elizabeth.
*Courtesy of the Little Bighorn Battlefield
National Monument*

Friends and family gather at the Custers' quarters at Fort Lincoln, November 1873. George stands third from the left; 2nd Lt. Benjamin Hodge stands between Custer and his wife, Elizabeth. *Courtesy of the Little Bighorn Battlefield National Monument*

Custers' quarters, Fort Lincoln, July 1875. From left, top row: Leonard Swett, Mrs. Elizabeth Bacon Custer, Mrs. Margaret Calhoun, Lt. James Calhoun; second row: W.C. Curtis, Second Lt. Richard E. Thompson, and Miss Emma Wadsworth; bottom row: 1st Lt. Thomas W. Custer, Miss Nellie Wadsworth, and Lt. Col. George A. Custer. *Courtesy of Elizabeth Custer Library and Museum at Garryowen, Montana*

A column of cavalry, artillery, and wagons travel across the plains on the Yellowstone Expedition 1873.
Courtesy of the National Archives & Records Administration 111-SC-98500

Custer Monument at his birthplace, New Rumsley, Ohio
Courtesy of the Little Bighorn Battlefield National Monument

Scene of General Custer's Land Stand. A pile of horse bones was all that remained, July 1877.
Courtesy of the National Archives & Records Administration 111-SC-82866

Northern Pacific Railroad tickets issued to George Custer and his wife, Elizabeth Bacon Custer, found in Custer's trunk after his death
Courtesy of Elizabeth Custer Library and Museum at Garryowen, Montana

Elizabeth Bacon Custer in mourning attire
Courtesy of Elizabeth Custer Library and Museum at Garryowen, Montana

Midway through the sojourn, the 7th Cavalry came upon a Sioux Indian village. According to Elizabeth, "Their lodges were in a circle and their ponies were inside the enclosure." Two Bears, the chief of the tribe, met George and the other officers as they approached, and they greeted one another with respect and kindness. Elizabeth was granted the honor of being presented to the chief's daughter. She joined the maiden in her tepee. "Her feet were moccasined," Elizabeth noted in her journal. "Her legs and ankles [were] wound round with beaded leggings, and she had on the buckskin garment which never varies in cut through all the tribes. A blanket drawn over her head was belted at the waist. To crown all this, however, she had an open parasol, brought to her, doubtless, as a present by some Indian returning from a council at Washington."[8]

After a few days with the Sioux, the cavalry pressed on to Fort Sully, a post midway between Yankton and Bismarck. The post was neatly kept and growing in size. There were twenty buildings, including a school, a library, multiple vegetable gardens, an area for the numerous livestock, and a parade ground. The Custers were treated to a special meal, given fresh supplies, and sent on their way.[9]

Not every Indian chief in the area was as welcoming as Two Bears. At times the troops came across stakes that had been driven into the ground with bits of red flannel and locks of hair attached to them. Indian warriors placed the stakes along the trail to frighten white settlers and soldiers, and prevent them from intruding any farther onto their land. Occasionally, Elizabeth would catch a glimpse of warring braves with painted faces closely watching her as she and the 7th Cavalry passed. George was mindful of how dangerous the trek was, and suggested to his wife that in the future, he should not subject her to such fear and worry. "It is infinitely worse to be left behind," she told him, "a prey to all the horrors of imagining what may be happening to [the] one we love."[10]

The caravan as a whole periodically stopped at the bends of the Missouri River to bathe, wash their clothes, and fish. Elizabeth would sit in the shade of a tree, watching George attempt to catch something for their evening meal. He made this an occasion to compete with other soldiers and lay a wager on who could catch the most fish.[11] Although the 7th Cavalry enjoyed short moments of rest from the grueling march, they never let their guard down. Hostile Indians lurked in the brush and plateaus overlooking the military's entire route.

By June 10, 1873, the troops were reaching the end of their expedition. The termination of the trip would be bittersweet for Elizabeth. "I regretted each day that brought us nearer the conclusion of our journey," she recalled in her memoirs. "For though I had been frightened by Indians, and though we had encountered cold, storms, and rough life, the pleasures of the trip over, balanced the discomforts."[12]

The Custers and the cavalrymen were given a warm welcome when they finally made it to Fort Rice. The other officer's wife was treated kindly as well. Elizabeth's personal belongings and those of the other woman did not make the trip unharmed. Their clothes, pictures, and books were mildewed and ruined by the rain and water that had seeped onboard the boat from the river. Elizabeth noted that she managed to maintain her composure until she saw the damage to her wedding dress, and then she burst into tears. Annoyed by the loss of his personal items as well, George held himself together by repeating the saying he had learned as a boy: "Never cry for spilled milk."[13]

Ten days after the Custers had arrived at Fort Rice, more than 15,000 cavalrymen, including George and his staff, were given orders to accompany a survey party for the Northern Pacific Railroad into the Northwest. George was one of the officers assigned to lead the way and protect the railroad crew from hostile Indians. Wives would not be allowed to go along with the troops on the Yellowstone Expedition, and there would be no exceptions.[14] Elizabeth wasn't happy with the decision and pleaded with General Stanley to at least let the women remain at Fort Rice. She believed letters from George would reach her more quickly if she stayed put. Had there been adequate housing for dependents, she might have been able to convince the powers that be to do just that.[15] Disappointed, because she had thought Fort Rice was going to be their new home, Elizabeth would have to return to Monroe, Michigan, to wait for word from George.

On June 20, 1873, George and his command left the post to begin the Yellowstone Expedition. Adorned in a bright red shirt, handmade by Elizabeth, George urged his mount in the direction of the Yellowstone River. Elizabeth tearfully waved good-bye. Benteen relished the fact that the devoted couple would be separated. He believed that they had no scruples and that superior officers gave them preferential treatment. After seeing her husband off, Elizabeth returned to Monroe to wait for George to complete the five-hundred-mile trek.[16]

Not long after the expedition began, George and General Stanley were at odds. George had hired a civilian trader named Balarian to accompany the troops into the field. The trader brought along two wagon trains filled with supplies, including alcohol. Balarian had been in trouble for selling whiskey to soldiers at Fort Rice, and Stanley had fired him and ordered him off the post. George disagreed with Stanley's decision and rehired the merchant, insisting that liquor in moderation was good for the morale of the troops. Stanley was furious that his authority had been challenged and warned George that future acts of defiance would not be tolerated.[17]

George paid little attention to his superior officer and seldom mentioned any problems with Stanley in his letters to Elizabeth. Instead, he wrote to her about the magnificent opportunities for hunting and how proud he was of the 7th Cavalry, boasting that his staff hadn't been intoxicated since the journey began. Not everyone on the expedition managed to avoid getting drunk, however. Several of George's fellow officers succumbed to alcohol, including Stanley himself. Stanley's drinking proved problematic for George. According to George, alcohol made the commander "act badly." He punished George whenever he thought the brash soldier was overstepping his authority and even moved Custer's regiment to the tail end of the caravan.

Benteen encouraged Stanley's scolding of George and reported anything he perceived to be an abuse of power. Benteen accused George of giving a cavalry horse to a civilian, and of sleeping with Eliza Brown Denison, a cook with the regiment.[18] When the chief engineer for the Northern Pacific survey crew heard the gossip and saw the treatment George and his troops were receiving, he demanded that a skilled cavalryman like Custer be allowed to take the lead of the expedition. The chief engineer argued that George and his men were supposed to be looking for warring Indians and not lingering behind, waiting to be ambushed. Stanley took exception to the survey crew leader's demands, but reluctantly ordered George back to the head of the tour.[19] Although Stanley never learned to like George, he respected the way Custer had dealt with the public reprimands and punishment he had issued, and the efficiency with which he had led his troops through the uncharted Dakota Territory. He would eventually apologize to George for his behavior. Benteen's claims that George stole a horse and was sleeping with Eliza Brown were considered gossip and were not investigated. The troops were preoccupied with the Yellowstone Expedition, and the subject was not brought up again.[20]

The lengthy letters George sent to Elizabeth made her homesick for life in tents and in the uncharted frontier. She busied herself with mundane domestic tasks and regularly attended church. She and George's sister, Margaret Calhoun, indulged in the occasional square dances and played parlor games with friends. Elliot Bates, one of Elizabeth's admirers from her days before George, frequently visited and enjoyed long conversations about the military and growing up in Monroe. She enjoyed his company, but was mindful of the length of time they spent together. She did not want friends or neighbors to think she was behaving inappropriately. "I am anxious to be above suspicion or reproach," Elizabeth wrote to George in July 1873. "I try to improve to be worthy of you," she added.[21]

Elizabeth admitted to merely "existing" between letters from George and news of his expedition. As soon as he and his troops reached the Yellowstone River in the territory of Montana, George sent word that he had arrived and was safe. "How I have longed for you during our march," he confessed in a letter dated July 19, 1873.[22] He described the landscape around him as "a Wonderland." He assured her that the railroad surveyors were doing their jobs without interference from Indians in the area, but their peaceful demeanor did not last long. The Indians were simply waiting for a reason to strike out at the army and railroad employees.[23]

General Stanley's ongoing episodes of drunkenness forced George to assume command of the entire expedition. With two companies in tow, he made his way to the Yellowstone River to rendezvous with a steamer carrying fresh provisions for the troops, necessary in order for them to continue on their journey. After establishing a makeshift supply depot on the south bank of the river, George traveled northwest in the direction of the Musselshell River.[24] Benteen, along with two companies, were left behind to guard the supply depot. Having to follow George's orders infuriated him, and Benteen complained that the only way Custer could have gotten away with being leader at the time was that "Stanley was stupidly drunk."[25]

By mid-August 1873, reports in the Associated Press alerted Elizabeth to the problems the 7th Cavalry was experiencing. The news was in sharp contrast to the information she had received from George. In between letters, Sioux warriors had attacked the soldiers because they had dared to venture onto a stretch of their sacred land. George and his men quickly retreated from the area, regrouped, and charged the Indians. The braves scattered across the prairie. With the exception of two men—veterinarian Dr. John Holzinger and Balarian, the civilian trader who supplied the alcohol to the troops—the cavalry survived the assault.[26]

The executives with the Northern Pacific Railroad praised George's leadership skills and credited his fearless direction for helping their survey crew to achieve their objective. "My little durl [sic] never saw people more enthusiastic over the 7th and her dear Bo than are the representatives of the R.R.," George wrote to Elizabeth after returning to the supply depot.[27] The military celebrated his efforts as well. George was made commander of a new post being built specifically to oversee the railroad's interests. He was also put in charge of the Middle District of the Department of Dakota, which included three other Missouri River posts. George sent word to Elizabeth to be prepared to move to Fort Abraham Lincoln in what is now central North Dakota. He would meet her in Monroe and escort her to their new home.[28]

The Custers arrived at the newly completed post in November 1873. George's brother Tom escorted them to their quarters, where the regimental band was waiting to welcome them. They played two of George's favorite tunes, "Home Sweet Home" and "Garryowen," the unofficial marching song of the 7th Cavalry. Elizabeth described the pristine camp in her memoirs as being located in a spectacular valley, "[w]hile just back of us stretched a long chain of bluffs . . . on the summit of a hill, nearly a mile to the left, was a small garrison. . . ."[29]

George and Elizabeth quickly settled into their elegant home, which had been built with every modern convenience available to the army. Instead of the standard hooks to hang clothes on, the commander's quarters featured several wardrobes. There was also a basement under the house for cold storage. The Custers spent a great deal of their time in the parlor, where they both kept busy writing. George worked on various articles for *Galaxy* magazine, with an eye toward writing a book, and Elizabeth was adding to her own memoirs.[30]

In the evenings, the Custers either entertained George's staff, their wives, and friends at their home, or at a special house constructed for theatrical presentations. According to Elizabeth's journal, the meeting house was a crude structure, but big enough to accommodate the Custers' usual group of followers. "The unseasoned cottonwood warped even while the house was being built," she recalled in her book *Boots and Saddles*, "but by patching and lining with old torn tents, they managed to keep out the storm. The scenery was painted on condemned canvas stretched on a frame-work, and was lifted on and off as the plays required. The footlights in front of the rude stage were tallow candles that smoked and sputtered inside the clumsy cobbled casing of tin. The seats and narrow benches [were] without backs."[31] The weekly shows featured clog-dancing and other song-and-dance routines. Enlisted men performed various roles in the original plays presented, and George would occasionally take on an acting part.

The entertainment available to Benteen, his wife, Catherine, and his staff at Fort Rice was woefully lacking. What little they had was presented at a converted sawmill. Soldiers serving under Benteen read and reread the same dozen or so books and magazines. Cavalrymen under Benteen's command, such as Tom Custer and First Lieutenant Edwin Mathey, escaped the bleak setting at Fort Rice to visit Fort Lincoln whenever they had detached duty. Benteen considered their actions disloyal and never shied away from making his feelings known. The men asked to be transferred to George's command, but Benteen denied their requests, steadfastly refusing to do anything that would benefit Custer. Benteen frequently complained about George being given choice commands and outposts over him and his supporters, and included Elizabeth in his common gripes as well.[32]

Elizabeth knew how Benteen felt about her and cringed whenever he came to Fort Lincoln. George prevailed upon her to set aside any bitterness and to be hospitable, and as the commanding officer's wife, she did so.[33]

The relatively quiet life the Custers had lived for eight months in Dakota Territory was interrupted in the summer of 1874 when the United States government ordered an expedition into the Black Hills. Political leaders had been bombarded with reports that Sioux Indians were killing white travelers who trespassed on their territory. The feeling among the officials at the Department of the Missouri was that something had to be done to stop the attacks. In truth, many professional hunters were encroaching on Indian land and thereby breaking the treaties the U.S. government had made with them. General Philip Sheridan, head of the Department of the Missouri, directed George to organize a force to explore the area. Although the mission was deemed "peaceful," the underlying objective was to find a spot suitable for a fort.[34]

On July 2, 1874, George left Fort Abraham Lincoln for the Black Hills. In his command were ten troops of 7th Cavalry soldiers, two companies of infantry, and a photographer named William H. Illingworth.*

Within the first day the trip had already exceeded George's expectations. "We have discovered a rich and beautiful country," he wrote to Elizabeth soon after he had left her. "[W]e have found gold and probably other valuable metals."[35] Although she wasn't sure when or if George would receive her letters, Elizabeth wrote to her husband faithfully.[36] She and the other women at the post kept watch for Indians who might try to overtake the camp in retaliation

---

* William H. Illingworth produced about seventy glass plates, including sixty of the Black Hills landscape and its features, and members of the 7th Cavalry.

for the wrongs that had been done to them. "I do not think the actual fear of death was thought of so much as the all absorbing terror of capture," she recorded in her memoirs. "Our regiment had rescued some white women from captivity in Kansas, and we never forgot the stories. One of our number became so convinced that their fate awaited us that she called a resolute woman to one side to implore her to promise that, when the Indians came into the post, she would put a bullet through her heart before she carried out her determination to shoot herself."[37]

The soldiers and dependents at Fort Abraham Lincoln were never in danger of being overcome, but George and the 7th Cavalry troops in the field believed they might be. Indians were seen watching the men make camp and following them from location to location; then, they would send up smoke signals to alert the other members of the tribe as to the army's travels. Although the Indians kept a respectable distance from George and his troops, they were deeply bothered by their presence in the west.

Illingworth, the photographer who accompanied the group, took copious stereoscopic pictures of the countryside. The scientists with the expedition maintained detailed records of the journey, noting the types of wildlife and plant life they found, as well as specifics about dinosaur bones that were discovered.[38]

George, a qualified taxidermist, collected various animals such as rattlesnakes, jackrabbits, an eagle, and an owl for his own menagerie. He also tracked and killed a bear, something he had been hoping to do from the onset of the trip. "I have reached the hunter's highest round of fame," he wrote to Elizabeth on August 15, 1874. "I have killed my Grizzly." He also instructed Elizabeth to gather all the press notices of the expedition that she came across.[39]

When the 7th Cavalry returned to Fort Lincoln on August 30, 1874, their wives and family were thrilled to have them home. Elizabeth noted in her memoirs that she was "wild with joy" to see George. Not unlike the other men on the expedition, his face was sunburned, his beard was heavy, and his clothes were patched and faded. Besides animal skins, pieces of gold and mica, and pressed flowers, George also brought Elizabeth a keg of water from a mountain stream.[40]

Benteen watched in disgust as George was hailed by the troops and a few members of the press as an explorer and discoverer of gold. Benteen's hatred for George had deepened during the expedition. He objected to the decisions Custer had made, to not stop the march and bury two soldiers who had passed away on the journey. Had it not been for Benteen, the men's bodies would have been left exposed on the trail. After George dismissed him at the conclusion of the trek, Benteen returned to Fort Rice and immersed himself in his duties, and in the baseball team he had organized, called the Athletics. His hope was to eventually beat the Fort Lincoln team in a series of games. Benteen felt the loss would be a humbling experience for both George and Elizabeth.[41]

By October, the Custers were on the move again. This time, however, the excursion was more pleasure- than work-related. The work George did to help the Northern

Pacific Railroad resulted in free passage anywhere the trains ran. After a brief stop in Monroe, the Custers traveled to Chicago to attend a friend's wedding. Among the other guests in attendance were President Grant, his wife, and General Sheridan.[42]

In November 1874, George's book, *My Life on the Plains*, was published and in wide release, although Benteen had begun a rumor—meant to discredit Custer—that Elizabeth, a talented writer herself, had helped him to write the book, along with all of the articles subsequent to its publication. George had completed working on the material in November 1873 while he and Elizabeth were at Fort Lincoln. The 256-page volume included his experiences from his days at West Point, as well as the 7th Cavalry's winter campaign in 1867 and 1868.[43]

George and Elizabeth spent the bulk of the winter back at their home at Fort Lincoln. They whiled away the long cold days and nights with friends. They rented a piano and sang war songs and hymns, played games, talked about their experiences together, and doted on the dogs they owned. "We were happy because we were together," Elizabeth recalled in her memoirs. When George was asked why he loved his wife, he quoted a line from a book by Harriet Beecher Stowe, entitled *My Wife and I*. "Because she never tries me," he said, "she never makes me nervous . . . if husbands and wives bore that proof successfully as time advanced they might count on a happy future."[44]

George had many qualities Elizabeth admired as well. One such commendable characteristic was his empathy for

Indians. "Love of country is almost a religion with them," he once said in an interview. "It is not the value of the land that they consider; but there is a strong local attachment that the white man does not feel, and consequently does not respect. . . ." Some of the Sioux Indian leaders recognized his understanding of their plight and sought his counsel on many occasions. They shared their concerns about the invasion of the white man and how they were being taken advantage of by greedy, dishonest Indian agents. Elizabeth noted with pride in her memoirs that George "was a sincere friend of the reservation Indian. He aided them as much as he could."[45]

Sensitive as he was to the Indians' situation, he would not tolerate any disrespect toward the people in his command. When George was informed that an Indian named Rain-in-the-Face was bragging about being the one who had killed the two men with the Yellowstone Expedition of 1873, he ordered a pair of his officers to apprehend the Indian. Captains Tom Custer and George Yates left the camp with a hundred troops to track and catch Rain-in-the-Face. Tom was the one who captured the Indian, having recognized him at a trader's store, fifty miles away from Fort Lincoln.[46]

The Dakota winter of 1874 and 1875 was long and far too sedate for George. Outside of monitoring the gold seekers pouring into the Black Hills, there was nothing but routine duties to occupy his time. In the spring he headed for New York to solicit businessmen to invest in the development of a mine. On his way back to Fort Lincoln, he made a stop in

Michigan. While in Monroe visiting relatives, he met with friends of the family, the Wadsworth sisters. Emma and Nellie were effervescent and exciting.[47] Although he escorted both of the lively sisters around town and to various community dances, he and Nellie were soon smitten with one another. He found her to be refreshing, and invited both Nellie and Emma to accompany him to Fort Lincoln for a visit. The women happily complied.[48]

Elizabeth kept herself busy while waiting for her husband's return. She spent time writing, playing cards, and taking walks with either Tom Custer or Thomas Weir. Blissfully unaware that Nellie and George were mutually attracted, she cheerfully welcomed the women into their home. Elizabeth was pleased to have the sisters at the post because there were so few single women available to talk to and mingle with the unattached soldiers on the post. She believed in matrimony as a savior of young officers. She thought if soldiers were married they would be less likely to succumb to the temptation to drink.[49] She hoped that the Wadsworth sisters would find their matches at the post.

In the summer of 1875, George and Elizabeth were preoccupied with making things ready for a visit from the secretary of war, William W. Belknap.[50] Elizabeth got their living quarters in pristine order, while George and the members of the 7th Cavalry cleaned and polished the camp. George was less than enthusiastic about the impending visit because he did not care for Belknap. He suspected the secretary was corrupt and taking bribes from post trading stores that charged soldiers exorbitant prices for supplies.

In fact, an investigation of President Grant's entire administration, including the secretary of war, was under way in Washington.[51]

George forced himself to be civil to Secretary Belknap when he arrived. He followed the military protocol, ordering the troops to salute the politician as he inspected the ranks, but he would not extend himself beyond that. Belknap left the camp insulted by George's behavior.[52]

Shortly after Belknap's exit, the Custers decided to take a trip to New York. Both longed for the nonstop activity available in a big city. They were flooded with invitations to parties and theatrical openings. They celebrated the thirteenth anniversary of their first meeting at their favorite eatery.[53] They discussed the life they had enjoyed together and their plans for the years to come.

There was a sense of foreboding that loomed over their evening together, however; like ants on a jelly sandwich, hordes of white settlers had flooded into the Black Hills, and the government and army were unable to stem the tide. Indian chiefs Black Moon, Sitting Bull, Gall, and Crazy Horse were organizing their tribes to protest the breaking of treaties.[54] The unrest in the West, combined with the ongoing probe into the mismanagement of military funds, prompted George and Elizabeth to question how long it would be before they again had an opportunity to spend time alone together.[55] The couple ended their meal reflecting on the times they had spent lounging about George's library at Fort Lincoln. "An idolizing wife could not live without you," Elizabeth told her husband.[56]

CHAPTER NINE

LOSING GEORGE

Indescribable yearning for the absent, and untold terror
for their safety, engrossed each heart.

—ELIZABETH CUSTER ON WAITING TO HEAR NEWS ABOUT THE FATE OF
GEORGE AND THE MEMBERS OF HIS COMMAND, 1885

It was almost two in the morning, and Elizabeth couldn't sleep. It was the heat that kept her awake, the sweltering, intense heat that had overtaken Fort Lincoln earlier that day, and now made even sleeping an uncomfortable prospect. Even if the conditions for slumber were more congenial, sleep would have eluded Elizabeth. The rumor that had swept through the army post around lunchtime disturbed her greatly, and until it was confirmed, she doubted that she'd ever be able to get a moment's rest.[1]

Elizabeth walked over to the window and gazed out at the night sky. It had been more than two weeks since she had said good-bye to her husband. She had left him and his troops a few miles outside of Fort Lincoln. His orders were to intercept the Sioux and Cheyenne Indians in the territory, force them back to the reservation, and bring about stability in the hills of Montana.[2]

Just before they rode out, she had turned around for one last glance at General George Custer's departing column. It was a splendid picture: The flags and pennants were flying, the men were waving, and even the horses seemed to be preening, showing how fine and fit they were. George rode to the top of a promontory and turned around, stood up in his stirrups, and waved his hat. Then they all started forward again, and in a few seconds, they had disappeared—men, horses, flags, and ammunition—all on their way to the Little Bighorn River.[3]

Over and over again she played out the events of the hot day that had made her so restless. Elizabeth and several other wives had been sitting inside her quarters, singing hymns, in the desperate hope that the lyrics would give comfort to their longing hearts. All at once they noticed a group of soldiers congregating and talking excitedly.[4] One of the Indian scouts, Horn Toad, ran to them and announced, "Custer killed. Whole command killed." The women stared back at Horn Toad in stunned silence. Catherine Benteen asked the Indian how he knew that Custer had been killed. He replied: "Speckled Cock, Indian Scout, just come. Rode pony many miles. Pony tired. Indian tired. Say Custer shoot himself at end. Say all dead."[5]

Elizabeth considered what one of the wives had reminded her about not putting much stock in hearsay. Their husbands had repeatedly warned them not to believe in rumors. Elizabeth believed there might have been a skirmish, but felt it unlikely that an entire command could be lost. At that moment she had refused to believe George would ever dare die. She would wait for confirmation before she did anything else. Now, in her bedroom, listening to the chirping of the crickets and the howls of the coyotes, she sat up, wide awake, waiting.[6]

The loud sound of boots tromping across the path toward her front door gave her a start. She hurried to the door and threw it open. Captain William S. McCaskey entered her home, followed by the post surgeon, Dr. J. Middleton, and Lieutenant C. Gurley, of the 6th Infantry. Captain McCaskey held his hat in his hands. He clearly didn't want to be there. Elizabeth looked at him, her eyes pleading.

"None wounded, none missing, all dead," he sadly reported.

Elizabeth stood frozen for a moment, unable to move, the color drained from her face.[7]

"I'm sorry, Mrs. Custer," the captain said, sighing. "Do you need to sit down?"

Elizabeth blinked away the tears. "No," she replied. "What about the other wives?" she asked.

"We'll let them know of their husbands' fate," he assured her.

Despite the intense heat, Elizabeth was now shivering. She picked up a nearby wrap and placed it around her shoulders. Her hands were shaking. "I'm coming with you," she said, choking back her tears. "As the wife of the post commander, it's my duty to go along with you when you tell the other . . . widows."

The captain didn't argue with the bereaved woman. He knew it would be pointless. Elizabeth was as stubborn as George, if not more so.[8]

Six months prior to the Battle of the Little Bighorn, George, along with more than forty miners, had been digging through a deep layer of snow that had blanketed the railroad tracks leading to Fort Lincoln. Elizabeth anxiously watched the men from her car window, noting that the drifts on either side of the train were as high as the vehicle itself. Harsh winds blew the loose, white powder off the mounds and back onto the path that had been so painstakingly forged.[9]

George and the other men wielding shovels were exhausted and cold. The train that had been inching steadily behind them came to a standstill when more snow relentlessly dropped from the sky.

Elizabeth lowered the window she was peering out of and caught a glimpse of a stage in the near distance. Slowly but surely, the vehicle approached the railroad engine, now lodged in a bed of ice. When the stage came into full view, Elizabeth recognized the man seated next to the capable driver as her brother-in-law Tom. As soon as the stage reached the train, Tom jumped down from the top and Thomas Weir stepped out of the cab.[10]

After receiving word that George and Elizabeth were held up en route due to a storm, the soldiers had hired a stage and driver out of Bismarck to meet the helpless train. They brought along an ample supply of food, warm clothing, and blankets for the continuation of the trip to George's post. "When at last I saw the light shining out of our door at Fort Lincoln, I could not speak for joy and gratitude at our release from such peril," Elizabeth recalled in her memoirs. "No light ever seemed so bright, no haven ever so blessed, as our own fireside. The train remained in the spot where we left it until the sun of the next spring melted down the great ice banks and set free the buried engine."[11]

Over the winter, the Custers had basked in the warmth of their quarters, recounting the perilous journey with friends and discussing what the future held. Elizabeth hoped to write a book, and George had plans to join a lecture circuit. An agency in New York had offered him a contract to tour the States and share his frontier experiences with ticket buyers. The tour was to begin in 1876 and run for four months. George would earn $200 a lecture and give five lectures a week. All of his and Elizabeth's expenses would be covered as well. George had requested that the tour be postponed until he had time to prepare. He hoped to be ready by the spring of 1877.[12]

Then, just as the Custers had finally thawed out from their frigid trek across the Northeast, George had been given orders to return to the nation's capital.[13] He speculated that he was needed back in Washington to discuss the army's idea of adding military posts along the Yellowstone River. George wanted to wait until he'd had a chance to run his troops through the proper training necessary to participate in the coming struggle against the Plains Indians, who wanted to stay on their ancestral land. He knew the Indians were going to have to be forced to return to the reservation and anticipated some resistance. His troops had to be ready.[14] General Alfred Howe Terry, commander of the Fort Lincoln Expedition, agreed with George regarding the training his troops needed and petitioned his superiors to postpone their meeting with Custer. He argued that George's experience in the field made him a valuable asset to the ensuing campaign. His request was denied.

The thought of traveling over the same frozen ground they had just covered did not excite Elizabeth, but she wanted to go with George. Not wanting Elizabeth to endure any more chilly scenes, he refused to allow her to accompany him.[15] George left for Washington, D.C., on March 14, 1876.

Before leaving, George told Elizabeth that he hoped to have an opportunity to further expand on the reports he had made to the government about some of the unscrupulous agents assigned to represent the reservation Indians. In addition to the agents stealing supplies that were meant to be given to the Indians, George was aware that many promises made to the Indians had been broken. He agreed with Chief Crazy Horse and Red Cloud, who pointed out to the soldiers that the white leaders could not stop white men from coming onto their land to dig for gold and silver.[16] George thought he could bring about change if he explained to the government that in order to establish peace on the Western frontier, it was crucial for white men to be as good as their word. "Whites or Indians committing wrongs are to be punished according to the law," George wrote in his biography, *My Life on the Plains*.[17]

It wasn't until George reached Washington, D.C., that he learned why he had been called back so abruptly. An investigation into the misappropriation of military funds and fraud had been launched by Hiester Clymer, chairman of the Committee on Expenditures in the Department of War, against members of President Ulysses S. Grant's cabinet. Having previously submitted information on what he knew about such illegal activities at Fort Lincoln, George was asked to testify. At the heart of the controversy was William W. Belknap, the secretary of war, and one of President Grant's most trusted cabinet members. Clymer had proof of Belknap's involvement and was seeking to have him impeached.[18]

On April 1, 1876, George hastily wrote to Elizabeth to inform her of what was happening. He noted in his letter that he had tried to visit with the president to ask to be returned to his post, but Grant, who felt betrayed by George's participating in the inquiry, would not see him.[19]

George's presence in Washington was front-page news. "I have been the recipient of kindest attentions from all papers except a few radicals," George informed Elizabeth. "I am surprised if a morning passes without abuse of myself. But leading papers throughout the country commend my courage."[20] Although the president rebuffed the decorated soldier, many others were pleased to have him back in town. He was inundated with dinner invitations and visits from friends and colleagues. George's social engagements were newsworthy as well. Reporters followed him to military balls and theater openings, and wherever he went, he was in the company of adoring women. He couldn't help admiring some of the women who sought him out. Sometimes the playful flirtation between George and the women he met led to potentially embarrassing situations, and journalists made note of the incidents. Such was the case with the popular artist and sculptor Vinnie Ream. After an evening of revelry with his friends and Miss Ream, George left his wallet at her home and had to retrieve it the following morning. He hoped Elizabeth would not get the wrong idea about the episode if it happened to be published in the newspapers the next day.[21]

George tried to keep his wife apprised of all of his activities, including any uncomfortable situations in which he found himself. Elizabeth pored over his letters and eagerly anticipated his homecoming. She kept him abreast of the events at the fort, particularly about how diligently the 7th Cavalry had been preparing for whatever lay ahead with the Indians.

Thomas Weir kept a sympathetic eye on Elizabeth. As he watched her, he recalled a letter he had written to George in August 1867 that expressed his devotion, not only to his commanding officer, but to George's wife as well. "Will any little favor I may be able to give be kindly received. I am anxious in the affair to go to your side." Elizabeth depended on Thomas's devotion. In George's absence, he escorted her to the limited social events held at the post.[22]

As expected, George's appearance before the committee on March 29, 1876, created quite a stir. He told the politicians about post traders he knew who were overcharging troops for supplies. He gave examples of extortion he had witnessed, and the testimony implicated Belknap in the illegal actions. Belknap's good friend, Orville Grant, President Grant's brother, was swept up in the scandal as well. Orville was a businessman who sold alcohol and sundries to the military. His close association with the secretary of war and their under-the-table dealings were brought to light during the hearing.[23]

George's testimony further alienated him from President Grant, who was already annoyed with George because of what he had written in his book, *My Life on the Plains*, released two years prior to the committee's probe into military spending. The negative comments George made in the book about the president's Indian policy infuriated Grant, and since reading the book, Grant had been considering the best way to make George suffer for his actions. The Belknap situation would give the president the opportunity to put George in his place. Belknap insisted that George was fabricating the story about soldiers being overcharged at post trading stores and also claimed that George had written an article published with an anonymous byline that appeared in a prominent newspaper, accusing the secretary of war, Orville, and the president of malfeasance. George vehemently denied the allegations.[24]

Belknap responded with a letter about the matter to his staff on the Plains, which included the commander of the 7th Cavalry, General Alfred Terry. The letter was meant to discredit George and possibly have him reprimanded for insubordination. "I have a copy of General Custer's testimony," Belknap wrote, "and it surpasses everything in the way of testimony that I ever read. It is purely hearsay, and would stand in no court a moment. . . . As for myself, I have only to say that in time I shall be vindicated, and [I am] bearing the bitter attacks upon myself as best I may. I await the result not very patiently but with some faith."[25]

The committee investigating the illegal activities found that Belknap had acted dishonestly and planned to impeach him. At Grant's urging, Belknap decided to resign and spare the administration any further embarrassment.[26]

George did suffer as a result of his time on the witness stand. Not only did President Grant deny him another field command, but he also refused his request to rejoin his outfit at Fort Lincoln. George was relentless and continued to try to gain an audience with the president in an effort to change his mind. He did not want the Sioux Expedition to go on without him. He also worried that the Indians might be mobilizing their forces during this period of the army's inactivity. In anticipation of a showdown with the Indians, George had been recruiting soldiers for work on the Plains. "I have been instrumental in getting four companies up from the South," he wrote to Elizabeth in mid-April 1876. "General Banning [head of the Military Affairs Committee] has prepared a long speech on the issue shortly to come up: transferring the Indian Bureau to the War Department," George elaborated. "He took many arguments in favor of it from my book, but asked me not to mention this till afterwards, lest others might use it."[27]

News that George would be able to send for Elizabeth if he were delayed in Washington beyond April helped him endure another day away from Fort Lincoln and his men. Elizabeth was overjoyed by the prospect. Whatever the government decided with regard to George's future, she was pleased to know they would be able to see it through together.[28]

George wanted that too and grew increasingly impatient as he waited for the government to approve Elizabeth's coming to the capital or his return to his post. The frustrated officer decided to take matters into his own hands. He hurried to General William Tecumseh Sherman's office to inform him that he was going to ride out to the Dakota Territory camp. Sherman was in New York, but George made his plans known to the adjutant general and inspector. Within hours of delivering the news, he was off to Fort Lincoln.[29]

When Sherman learned of George's actions, he quickly sent a message to General Philip Sheridan in Chicago to stop the brash soldier when he transferred trains there. "Order him to halt and wait further orders," Sherman wrote. "Meanwhile, let the expedition from Fort Lincoln proceed without him." George was stunned and angry.[30]

When newspaper editors received word about how George was being treated, they accused President Grant of keeping him from his duties, "to deter other officers from telling what they knew" about other military scandals. George dispatched a letter to the commander in chief, pleading with him to reconsider. "I appeal to you as a soldier to spare me the humiliation of seeing my regiment march to meet the enemy and I not share its dangers," he wrote to President Grant. The president finally acquiesced and gave his consent for George to accompany the expedition.[31]

Frederick Benteen left Fort Rice for Fort Lincoln on May 5, 1876, the same day George departed for the post from Chicago. He was annoyed to learn that George would be leading the 7th Cavalry in the field. He had hoped the events in Washington would keep him out of the action altogether.[32] Elizabeth secretly harbored the same thought. A strange sense of foreboding had swept over the post. She had confidence in her husband's abilities as a soldier, but tragedy was in the air. She later recalled, "Although we had seen the men start out on many long campaigns in those seven years on the Plains, we knew this was different, and we all felt it might have very serious results."[33]

When George arrived at the camp on May 12, 1876, he brought with him his nephew and niece, Autie and Emma Reed. Other family members already at the post were his brothers, Tom and Boston, his sister, Margaret, and his brother-in-law, James Calhoun. In the few days leading up to the troops leaving for the Little Bighorn, the Custers enjoyed meals with their relatives and friends, and discussed the events that George had experienced in Washington, D.C.[34] Reveling in the good food and laughter helped alleviate some of the anxiety Elizabeth was feeling about the upcoming expedition, at least for a little while.[35] George was confident and in high spirits,

Before dawn on May 17, 1876, George and six hundred members of the 7th Cavalry rode out of Fort Lincoln.

Elizabeth and her sister-in-law, Margaret Calhoun, were permitted to accompany the troops for the first day of the march. A band played "Garryowen" as they made their way past the post's main entrance. Twenty-seven Arikara Indians (a farming tribe whose homeland is in northern South Dakota) rode with the soldiers as scouts. As the regiment led its mounts around the Arikara Indian camp near the fort, the squaws and old men left behind began to chant. The Indian scouts echoed the tune Elizabeth recalled in her memoirs as "weird and melancholy beyond description. It is more of a lament or a dirge than an inspiration to activity."[36]

Although Elizabeth was troubled, George assured her that there was no need to worry. He reminded her that the intent of the expedition was to put a scare into the Sioux Indians that they'd never forget. To further put Elizabeth's mind at ease, George explained how certain he was of success. He reasoned that when the Sioux learned they were surrounded, they would surrender and proceed peacefully to the reservations. A thousand soldiers led by General George Crook were coming from the south, and General John Gibbon's troops would be coming from the north. The Crow Indians, who were government allies, would be waiting on the west. The 7th Cavalry would drive in from the east.[37]

George talked to his wife about meeting him in Yellowstone after the Indians had relented. Elizabeth listened intently as he described the beauty of the area and how they could explore the spectacular land together on horseback. Elizabeth nodded in agreement with his plan. He was so excited at the prospect, she could not bring herself to verbalize the qualms she had about him leaving.[38]

When morning came, Elizabeth and George said their good-byes. Dressed in a fringed buckskin suit and wearing a scarlet kerchief around his neck, George led the long blue column of soldiers on their way. Elizabeth stared pensively after him. "With my husband's departure my last happy days in [the] garrison were ended as a premonition of disaster that I had never known before weighed me down," she wrote in her memoirs. "I could not shake off the baleful influence of depressing thoughts. This presentiment and suspense, such as I had never known, made me selfish. I shut into my heart the most uncontrollable anxiety and could lighten no one else's burden."[39]

Elizabeth and George had exchanged a few letters as he made his way across the Plains. The correspondence was close at hand when the officers' wives and those of the enlisted men were informed of their spouses' fates. Elizabeth tucked them into the folds of her garment and held onto them tightly while the news was delivered.[40] Some of the grief-stricken women fell to the ground crying when they were told. Others stared blankly off into space, unable to comprehend the thought. Margaret Calhoun was nearly in hysterics at hearing that her husband, her brothers,

George, Tom, and Boston, and her nephew Henry Reed had perished. "Is there no message for me?" She wept. "Did they have a message for me?!"[41]

"At that very hour the fears that our tortured minds had portrayed in imagination were realities," Elizabeth noted in her journal, "and the souls of those we thought upon were ascending to meet their maker."[42]

CHAPTER TEN

SUDDENLY ALONE

Few men had more enemies than Custer, and no man deserved them less.

—FREDERICK WHITTAKER, AUTHOR, 1877

Persistent raindrops tapped against the windows of Elizabeth Custer's Park Avenue apartment in New York City. The prim, eighty-four-year-old woman, clad in a black, Edwardian dress, stared out at the dreary, foggy weather. She wore a pensive expression. Her graying hair was pulled back neatly into a tight bun, although a few loose tendrils had escaped and gently framed her small face. Her throat was modestly covered with lace.

The room around Elizabeth was grand in size and filled with items she had collected during her days on the Western Plains. Framed drawings of the Kansas prairie, a trunk with George's initials across the top, photographs of friends and family at various outposts, and an assortment of books on subjects ranging from travel beyond the Mississippi to the types of wildflowers that lined the Oregon Trail were among her treasures. The sparse furnishings in the apartment were covered with newspapers and journals. A small desk was littered with hundreds of letters.

Elizabeth glanced at the clock on a nearby table and then clicked on a radio housed in a gigantic cabinet beside her. As she tuned the dial through static and tones, a bright, maroon light from the console of the radio sifted into the hollow of the dark room. At the same time, the fog outside the window lifted a bit and the vague, misty outlines of palatial apartment buildings, museums, and churches came into view.

Elizabeth found the radio station she was looking for and leaned back in a plush chair as a voice described upcoming programming. She pulled a shawl around her shoulders and sat, patiently waiting. After a few moments an announcer broke in with pertinent information about the broadcast that Elizabeth planned to listen to: an episode of *Frontier Fighters*, entitled "Custer's Last Stand." The airdate was June 26, 1926, fifty years after the Battle of the Little Bighorn.[1]

As the audio reenactment unfolded, Elizabeth's eyes settled on a photograph of George hanging on the wall above the radio, and she remembered the awful moment when she'd first heard the news of George's death. She would never forget the devastated look on the faces of the twenty wives who had also lost their husbands that day. "From that time the life went out of the hearts of the women who wept," Elizabeth wrote in her memoirs, "and God asked them to walk on alone in the shadows."[2]

George Custer had underestimated the number of braves and warriors the 7th Cavalry would face at the Little Bighorn, as well as the Indians' zeal to defend a three-mile stretch of land along the Bighorn River. More than five thousand Indians stood that day against six hundred soldiers. George had divided his command into three detachments. Officers Marcus Reno and Frederick Benteen each had control of a unit. George took the lead of the third, in what would be his final charge into battle.[3]

Neither Reno nor Benteen came to his aid when he was surrounded and low on ammunition; in fact, Benteen disregarded George's orders to provide help. George's note to Benteen had read: "Come on. Big village. Be quick. Bring Packs. P.S. Bring Packs." Captain Thomas Weir, who was under Benteen's command, asked the officer for permission to assist George and the troops with him, but his request was denied.[4]

Soldiers in Benteen's and Reno's detachments who were wounded in battle were transported by steamer up the Bighorn and Little Bighorn Rivers to Fort Abraham Lincoln. Grieving family members who hoped the vessel would also be carrying the remains of their loved ones were disappointed. The bodies of the slain troops remained where they fell.[5] Official word of the tragic assault reached the public at large on July 7, 1876. Newspaper headlines all over the country conveyed the national shock and outrage, including one in the *Bethlehem Daily Times,* in Bethlehem, Pennsylvania, which read GENERAL CUSTER'S TERRIBLE DEFEAT. The short article that followed succinctly stated what had happened:

The defeat and massacre of General Custer and the five companies of cavalry with which he charged the camp of Sitting Bull in the Indian country are confirmed. It appears that his command and Reno's attacked the camp at different moments, losing the moral effect of a simultaneous attack. Major Reno lost 95 killed and wounded. General Custer's command was annihilated. An official report has been sent on by mail. The government has taken steps to intercept it, and cause its contents to be forwarded by telegraph. Sitting Bull, by whom General Custer's command was defeated, has been on the warpath for years, and has never assented to a treaty.[6]

The newspapers were slower to report that George's men had been scalped and mutilated by the Indians, although George's body had been left intact. He had a gunshot wound to the head and another in his side. He was buried where he fell along with the others at the Last Stand.[7]

Elizabeth held a service in the parlor of her quarters at Fort Lincoln. Widows, children, laundresses, and scouts attended. They remembered their loved ones in prayer, and with heavy hearts, they tried to sing hymns. They finally dispersed after reciting the Lord's Prayer. Elizabeth was so overcome with emotion that she fainted.[8]

Two weeks after the Battle of the Little Bighorn, Elizabeth and the other widows left the post. They were loaded into several of the 7th Cavalry's spring wagons, normally used to transport the dead, and escorted to the nearest train depot. From there Elizabeth proceeded to the place where it all began for her and George—Monroe, Michigan. During the long train ride she pored over letters from military personnel and political figures.[9] She also read various newspaper accounts of the fight. General Alfred Terry noted in his official reports that at noon on June 25, "He [Custer] found a village of almost unexampled extend, and at once attacked it with that portion of his force which was immediately at hand. . . . On the movement of General Custer and the five companies under his immediate command, scarcely anything is known from those who witnessed them, for no soldier or officer who accompanied him has yet been found alive."[10]

A number of Cheyenne women, such as Kate Big Head, claimed they had witnessed the scene, watching the battle from the western hills across the valley. According to their personal accounts, they insisted that the cavalry had hidden from the Indians behind their horses and that most of the troops, including George Custer, had shot themselves in the head because they were afraid of dying at the hands of the Indians.[11]

Elizabeth spent the majority of the trip to Michigan considering how she would go on without George. "I could only think of one thing," she wrote in her memoirs: "I wanted to die."[12]

During the journey back to her hometown, and after she had arrived at her father's house, well-meaning people offered their sympathies, but beyond the condolences, they had questions about George. People wanted to know what kind of man he truly was; what he thought of his superior officers; and what had really happened at the Battle of the Little Bighorn. Elizabeth had been pondering some of those questions herself. Military leaders were blaming George for the massacre, claiming that he had disobeyed orders. General Terry formally reported that George did not wait for another column of troops to arrive before pressing ahead to meet the Indians.[13] With few exceptions, George's most ardent critics cited his arrogance and independent thinking for the unnecessary loss of life. Reno told his superiors that among the many mistakes George had made was not taking Gatling guns with him when he left Fort Lincoln. Benteen referred to George's tactics on the battlefield as "senseless valley hunting ad infinitum."[14]

Elizabeth was outraged by the accusation that George had been derelict in his duty. She defended his leadership skills and praised him as a hero. Among those who championed George's actions were General George McClellan, Colonel James Forsyth, and Captain Thomas Weir.[15] Thomas was greatly troubled and guilt-ridden by what he'd witnessed at the battle scene. He felt his comrades, friends, and brothers in arms had been purposely betrayed.

Elizabeth received letters from all three supporters. McClellan reminded her that the same men who were now proclaiming that George had acted rashly would have also said he acted timidly if the Indians had escaped. Colonel Forsyth noted that George had followed the orders he'd been given and that he himself would not have done less.[16] Thomas's letter was heartbreaking and mysterious. He implied that Reno and Benteen had allowed George and his company to be killed. "I know if we were all of us alone in the parlor, at night, the curtains all drawn and everybody else asleep, one or the other would make me tell you everything," he wrote to Elizabeth. "If I can get away I am going to Monroe. I know I could say something to you all that would make you feel glad for a little while at least."[17]

As Elizabeth planned her husband's memorial service, a formal inquiry into the battle was being discussed. Reno was pushing the military to investigate the matter in an attempt to clear his name of any wrongdoing. In the interim he was placed in charge of the 7th Cavalry.[18]

The Methodist church where the Custer family memorial service was held on August 13, 1876, was packed with mourners and curious newspaper reporters. The faithful widow entered the sanctuary flanked on either side by her sister-in-law, Margaret Calhoun, and good friend, Annie Yates. The women sadly took their places in the front pews. All three had lost their spouses at Custer's Last Stand. After the hymn "I Would Not Live Always" was sung, the minister read the names of the men being memorialized: George Custer; his brothers, Tom and Boston; his brother-in-law, James Calhoun; his nephew, Harry Reed; and his comrade in arms, George W. Yates. The fallen were recognized for their bravery and courage under fire.[19]

The U.S. Congress officially recognized how much the Custer family had lost. George's parents had suffered the loss of three sons, a son-in-law, and a grandson. In order to help Emanuel and Maria Custer through this difficult time, a bill was passed authorizing a $50-per-month pension for the couple. Elizabeth was awarded the same amount. An additional bill was approved to donate a bronze cannon to be used in the eventual creation of a statue memorializing George.[20]

Elizabeth returned to her family home heartbroken and lonesome for her husband. She had yet to tackle the difficult job of going through George's personal belongings. The trunk he had carried with him from post to post, his uniforms, and his private notes and correspondence needed to be sorted through and organized. Before she began the difficult task, she reread a letter that her cousin, Rebecca Richmond, had sent to her shortly after George was killed. The letter was comforting to Elizabeth and gave her strength to face the forlorn days ahead. "Your life with Armstrong has been intense, concentrated, three or four, or a dozen ordinary lives in one," Rebecca had written on August 11, 1876, "and those who can live over again quietly, thoughtfully, and I will say pleasurably, be near you. Libbie, how much rather would you be the early widow of such a man than the life-long wife of many others!"[21]

Elizabeth painstakingly removed George's belongings from a leather footlocker and placed them reverently beside her on the floor. Two of the items were passes for travel on the Northern Pacific Railroad. One of the tickets was made out to General Custer and the other to Elizabeth. Among the newspaper clippings, animal hides, photographs, and tickets were letters from colleagues and relatives. Elizabeth casually leafed through thank-you notes, bulletins, and dispatches until she came across a love letter written in a hand she didn't recognize. "Dear General," the correspondence began, "Try and come down tonight if possible, for I have many things to say to you. Remember for I love you forever. Oh do not disappoint me. For the love of heaven burn this as soon as you read it and oblige your own loving Nellie."[22]

Elizabeth speculated that the author of the love letter was Nellie Wadsworth. Nellie and her sister Emma had spent time at the Custers' home at Fort Lincoln. George had brought the ladies with him to the post after visiting Monroe in 1875. Before returning the letter to George's footlocker, Elizabeth jotted the woman's name down on the back of the letter. She knew that it wasn't unusual for her husband to have had admirers, and of all the Nellies she and George had known, Nellie Wadsworth seemed the most likely candidate to have been involved with George.[23]

Elizabeth found other items of significant interest among George's things, including a life insurance policy worth $4,750 and an unpaid promissory note for $13,000. Knowing George as she did, the possibility that there were other unpaid debts was very likely. Elizabeth pondered her bleak financial situation. She had been awarded $900 from a widow's fund created by the *New York Herald* newspaper; $197 from the United States Treasury, for George's participation in the Belknap trial; and $500 from Grand Duke Alexis as a token of his sympathy.[24] After settling outstanding debts, helping support her elderly in-laws, and paying her moving expenses, Elizabeth had little left to pay for her own food, clothing, and shelter. The pension the government had agreed to pay her was appreciated, but would not cover her monthly bills. The thirty-four-year-old widow needed to find work.

Knowing there were few jobs that respectable women could pursue added to Elizabeth's anxiety. Coming to terms with the fact that George was gone and dealing at last with the very real possibility he had been unfaithful with more than one woman, including a family friend, made the process of moving on with life almost unbearable. On a scrap of onionskin paper Elizabeth jotted down what she believed was the only way she could get through the difficulties ahead and maintain her husband's reputation. In French she wrote, *Oublier! Oublier! C'est le secret de la vie.* ("To forget! To forget! It is the secret to life.")[25]

As the initial shock of the tragic events at the Little Bighorn subsided, Elizabeth became even more aware of the negative statements continually being made about her husband and his record as a soldier.[26] In several interviews, President Ulysses Grant claimed that George's military tactics were faulty and that he had willfully disobeyed orders. George had sent Elizabeth a copy of the orders he had been given and she knew he'd acted accordingly. "It is of course impossible to give you any definitive instructions," General Terry wrote to George prior to engaging the Indians in battle. "The Department Commander places too much confidence in your zeal, energy, and ability," Terry added, "to impress precise orders which might hamper your actions when nearly in contact with the enemy."[27]

Convinced that her husband had been in the right, Elizabeth set about to stop the speculation and to defend his honor. She pushed for military leaders and politicians to stop talking about launching an inquiry into the happenings at the Little Bighorn and to actually begin the much-needed hearings. Elizabeth also helped to organize fund-raising events and worked with committee chair members dedicated to building a monument in George's honor.[28]

In between the work she was doing to preserve her husband's good name, she was searching for a job. Elizabeth secured a part-time secretarial position with the New York Sanitary Commission, a government agency that raised money for veterans and their widows, and ran kitchens in army camps, soldier's homes, and homes for disabled veterans. Elizabeth's job entailed maintaining the incoming and outgoing letters for the organization and helping to collect donations.[29]

Elizabeth used any spare moment she had to write books about her life in the army with George, and her memoirs—*Boots and Saddles, Following the Guidon,* and *Tenting on the Plains*—sold well. She was highly sought after to give lectures about her experiences as a military wife.[30] Rumors of George's extramarital affairs insinuated themselves into various talks. Elizabeth was respectful of all inquiries, but never admitted any improprieties in public. A note she wrote to herself about life after the death of her controversial spouse explained the daunting task of managing George's legacy: "My motto is, Once a widow, always cautious—so difficult for a widow to preserve her reputation and enjoy the fleeting hours. Reputation is the result of caution. The paragraph of today wraps up the parcel of tomorrow. Everything but my stockings."[31]

Elizabeth received hundreds of letters of encouragement a day, some from suitors who had hoped at one time to marry her. Elliot Bates knew Elizabeth from childhood and was deeply in love with her. They had remained close even after she had married George. When news of George's death reached Elliot, he wrote to Elizabeth, expressing his sympathy and spurring her on in her endeavors. "Words are useless and I will not attempt to say anything, for I know that to you there is but one consolation. You bear the most honored widowhood of any woman who has ever married a cavalry officer in this country. For George Armstrong Custer was the best light cavalry officer we have ever had."[32]

Thomas Weir continued to reach out to Elizabeth, although his letters to her were more sorrowful and filled with regret over what he hadn't been allowed to do for the slain cavalrymen. "It is my business to vindicate my friends of that day," he wrote in November 1876. In another note he again informed Elizabeth that he had something of great importance to tell her. He promised to come and see her, to discuss the pressing issue on his heart and mind. Elizabeth looked forward to his visit.[33]

The first Thanksgiving Elizabeth spent without George was difficult. She kept herself busy, reviewing the ever-changing plans she had for George's monument—how it should look, what sculptor should be hired. An investigation into the Battle of the Little Bighorn was yet to get under way. The government's primary concern was dealing with the Indians who had led the charge against the 7th Cavalry. Warring chiefs and braves were hunted and killed. The Indians who surrendered were either jailed or moved to reservations.[34]

Elizabeth read dozens of magazine and newspaper accounts of the military campaigns against the Plains Indians. She was particularly fond of reports written by Frederick Whittaker, an author who had captured Elizabeth's attention with a eulogy he'd penned about George for *Galaxy Magazine*.[35] The London-born writer had met George at the magazine's editorial department in 1873. He was captivated by the general and his career, and infatuated with Elizabeth. Whittaker sought out 7th Cavalry soldiers, including Thomas Weir, who had championed George, and interviewed them for a series of articles. The published articles were highly critical of Marcus Reno and Frederick Benteen. Whittaker charged the two with cowardice and suggested they purposefully left George and his men to die. Elizabeth was resentful of Benteen's allegations against George and grateful for Whittaker's bold support.[36]

Thomas Weir appreciated Whittaker's work as well, but continued to be deeply shaken by his experience at the Little Bighorn. After the battle, Thomas returned to Fort Lincoln and continued with his duties until late November 1876, when orders from his commanding officer came through, requesting his presence on the East Coast. Thomas was sent on a recruiting mission to New York. By the time he arrived in the city, he was suffering from exposure, fatigue, and chronic depression. The physician who called on Thomas also noted he was extremely nervous and having trouble swallowing. Thomas remained in his room for days. An orderly periodically looked in on him. On December 9, the orderly found Thomas dead. A Western Union telegram sent to the adjutant general of the U.S. Army listed the cause of death as "congestion of the brain."[37]

Elizabeth was deeply affected by Thomas's death, and she wrote to the doctor attending him at the time of his passing. In a reply dated December 20, 1876, Doctor S. H. Orten informed Elizabeth that Thomas's death was due to melancholia. Coincidentally, the biography Whittaker had written about George Custer, entitled *The Complete Life of General George Custer*, was released the day Thomas died. Whittaker believed that Thomas's passing would prove to be beneficial for Reno and Benteen. He would never be able to share what he supposedly knew about their actions on June 25, 1876, with the politicians and military leaders presiding over the inquiry. Whittaker maintained in his book that Reno and Benteen willfully disobeyed orders, and if they had done as George asked, the Battle of the Little Bighorn might have been Custer's greatest victory.[38]

Benteen was outraged by Whittaker's claim. In a letter published in the *Army and Navy Journal*, Benteen expressed his belief that both Thomas and Elizabeth had biased the author with their inflated opinion of George and their common hatred for him. "None of them can bear the test of light and truth," Benteen noted, referring not only to Elizabeth and Thomas, but also all of the cavalrymen Whittaker had used to feed his scenario. "But still they have succeeded in getting vile slanders into public print," he added.[39]

In late September 1877, the bodies of the slain cavalrymen at the Little Bighorn were exhumed. Elizabeth made arrangements for George's remains to be sent to West Point. His reburial took place on October 10. George's flag-draped coffin was carried to a spot under a row of elm trees, a lone horse following the procession to the open grave.[40]

Elizabeth had little tolerance for any criticism leveled at her late husband. Regardless of his human frailties, which she strove to keep out of the public eye, in her estimation he remained a noble figure. She seized every invitation extended to her to speak about George's career and courageous life, and she was paid well for her lectures.

With encouragement from Whittaker and close friends and family, she never strayed from her main objective. Elizabeth wanted an official inquiry into the circumstances surrounding her husband's death, and for George to be recognized as a war hero.

Benteen spoke out against Elizabeth's aggressive push for an investigation and about the talks she was giving. In his opinion, the world should look upon George as a "full-fledged braying donkey rather than a 'martyr.'" Benteen wrote the following to historian David F. Barry in May 1897:

When one thinks seriously of it, it is quite sufficient to vex one that in the fiasco of the Battle of the Little Bighorn, from the fact that General Custer split his command of one regiment of cavalry into four separate and distinct columns, out of all communication with each other, with no orders of any kind, nor understanding even, that any of the separated columns were to receive support, even were such possible from the other, then with five troops under his own command to sally forth on an unknown trail—and in a direction that we never even guessed that he had gone until so informed by the chief Gall ten years after the occurrence of the battle—and in thirty minutes after his being attacked by the Indians, every man of Custer's five troops were slain. Isn't it easy, to say the least, somewhat vexatious that the balance of the command that stood off the horses of savages for two days that had easily annihilated Custer's command, to have been so grievously assailed by penny-a-liners and novel writers hunting for an early market for their wares? And in the case of Mrs. Custer, to keep the name of General Custer fresh in the memories of the public, that in her lectures to that generous public she may receive a fitting audience. Ah! The whole business is too patent and a simple money-making scheme.[41]

Elizabeth's persistent pleas to the government for an inquiry paid off in 1879. Her entire family attended the proceedings, which began in Chicago on January 13. Twenty-three witnesses, including Reno, were called. Reno was eager to take the stand and defend himself against any wrongdoing. Elizabeth and Whittaker maintained that he was guilty of not following George's orders on the battlefield. Reno took a verbal beating from fellow soldiers, who believed he had been indecisive and timid during the battle. A civilian traveling with Reno's company on the day of the event testified that the officer had been too drunk to lead. Benteen's behavior was also criticized by witnesses, although to a much lesser degree. After the court had carefully weighed all the testimony presented, it determined there was nothing in the officers' conduct that required any prosecutorial action.[42]

Elizabeth was disappointed with the outcome of the inquiry, but took comfort in what George had once said about similar unfair treatment he had experienced. "I don't believe a man ever perpetrated a rank injustice knowingly upon his fellow man but that he suffered for it before he died."[43]

By 1892, Elizabeth had become financially self-sufficient and used her income to build a home for herself in Bronxville, New York. In between book signings, literary club meetings, and lectures, she personally answered more than 300 cards and letters, received weekly, about George and their life together. She remained an outspoken advocate for his integrity. She never failed to compliment her late husband and boast about his daring and drive. She praised his military career and always placed the blame for his death and that of his company on Benteen and Reno. She lived to preserve his memory.[44]

Elizabeth worked tirelessly on the details involved with erecting statues of George on his grave in New York; in New Rumley, Ohio, where he was born; and in Monroe, Michigan, where he was raised. She traveled to Kansas

City, Missouri, to attend the unveiling of a painting done by prominent artist John Mulvany, of George and his men at the Last Stand. In November 1886, she was in the audience at Madison Square Garden to watch a reenactment of the Battle of the Little Bighorn, performed by Buffalo Bill Cody and his talented troupe of riders and sharpshooters. She loved Cody's portrayal of her husband and encouraged her friends to see the show.[45]

In an effort to further memorialize her husband's military accomplishments, Elizabeth contributed a number of articles to the *New York Sun* and *Century Magazine*. She wrote about garrison life, Plains living, buffalo hunting, and the people she and George had met during their travels.[46]

In addition to the trips Elizabeth made back and forth across the United States, speaking to the public about George and their life together, she also traveled abroad. She visited Europe, the Far East, Egypt, and Turkey, keeping detailed journals about her adventures. The journals included swatches of fabric from traditional garments and drawings of ancient ruins and the people who inhabited the lands. She was well received everywhere she went and acted as an unofficial ambassador for America.[47] No matter where she traveled, she never strayed far from the topic of George. She took on any author who dared publish a book that cast her husband in a negative light.

Elizabeth marked each anniversary of the Battle of the Little Bighorn by doing an interview with reporters about the hazards of living on the frontier and the courage of her protector husband. On the fifty-fifth anniversary of the famous Last Stand, Elizabeth declined to speak with the press, explaining, "I am not feeling up to the mark." Her niece told them Elizabeth was tired, and her health was failing.[48]

On April 2, 1933, George's widow suffered a heart attack. She passed away on April 4, just four days short of her ninety-first birthday. The news of her death was carried in every major publication around the world. The April 16, 1933, edition of the *Salt Lake Tribune* noted: "[I]n her passing another link with the colorful frontier days is severed. Up to the day of her death, Mrs. Custer's recollection of the stirring days of the Indian wars remained acute. For she was no stay-at-home soldier's wife in those days, but insisted on accompanying her husband on many of his campaigns."[49] The *San Antonio Express* echoed the sentiment and added, "In the early [1870s], when women were making their first demands for higher education and otherwise were preparing the way for their sisters of the twentieth century, young Elizabeth Custer also pioneered. She went west with her soldier-husband to share with him the hardships, dangers and thrills of post life on the Plains."[50]

Elizabeth's close friends and relatives celebrated her life at a service held at her Park Avenue apartment. She was laid to rest next to George at West Point on April 6, 1933. She was remembered by many as a woman of many talents, a loving aunt, and a fiercely devoted wife.[51] She had outlived all of George's key critics. Marcus Reno died on March 29, 1889, following surgery for cancer of the tongue at the age of fifty-four. Frederick Benteen died on June 17, 1898, of cerebral apoplexy at sixty-four. Even in his final days, Benteen never stopped berating George. "The newspapers killed Custer," he told an *Atlanta Journal* reporter. "They puffed him up and boosted him and sang his praises to the skies until it ruined him."[52]

Elizabeth's will, offered for probate on May 11, 1933, included instructions for a number of historical artifacts. Among the artifacts were two flags of truce used on the occasion of the surrender of General Lee at Appomattox. She left the flags to the United States government. A button owned by George Washington was left to West Point Academy.[53] Although not mentioned in the will, the May 12, 1933 edition of the *Salt Lake Tribune* reported that Elizabeth made monetary provisions for her two nieces as well.

Until the moment she drew her last breath, Elizabeth maintained that George was a patriot and a hero. "You are a positive use to your day and generation," she wrote to her husband just before the Battle of the Little Bighorn. "Do you not see that your life is precious on that account?"[54]

Appendix: The Last Will and Testament of Elizabeth Bacon Custer

George
I, ELIZABETH B. CUSTER, widow of General Armstrong Custer, of the Village of Bronxville, County of Westchester and State of New York, do hereby make, publish and declare this to be my Last Will and Testament, hereby revoking all wills by me at any time heretofore made.

FIRST: I direct that all my just debts and funeral expenses be paid as soon as possible after my decease, and that all inheritance, transfer, estate and succession taxes be paid out of my general estate.

SECOND: The two flags of truce, one made of a white towel and the other of a white handkerchief, which were used on the occasion of the surrender of General Lee at Appomattox, and also the table on which the surrender of General Lee to General Grant was written, and which are owned by me and now located in the Memorial Hall of the War Department Building in Washington, D.C., I give and bequeath to the UNITED STATES GOVERNMENT, in the hope that they may be permitted to retain their present position.

THIRD: A button owned by me and said to be cut from one of the coats of George Washington and given to my late husband by the mother of James B. Washington, a class mate from Virginia of General Custer's at West Point in the Class of 1861, I give and bequeath to the UNITED STATES MILITARY ACADEMY at West Point, or to whatever authority may be proper.

FOURTH: My husband's portraits and photographs, his arms, accoutrements, uniforms, souvenirs of war or frontier, books and illustrations, trophies of the chase, and each and every article of personal property owned by me, which is or may be considered in any way a souvenir of my late husband, General George Armstrong Custer, the question as to whether any particular item does or does not fall within the category of a souvenir to be absolutely and finally determined by my Executor, I give to my Executor with instructions to deliver the same over to the Public Museum or Memorial which may be erected on the battlefield of the Little Big Horn in Montana, if any, prior to my death, or which may be erected on said battlefield within the lives of Elizabeth E. Wellington, of Bronxville, N.Y., and May Custer Elmer, wife of Charles E. Elmer, of 14 Clark Street, Brooklyn, New York, and if not then to any historical museum or museums anywhere which may be selected by my Executor, or said Executor can deliver such articles as to it may seem proper as souvenirs to my personal friends or to any relative of General George Armstrong Custer. I suggest that in connection with the disposition of the articles mentioned in this Clause of my Will my Executor consult with one or more of the following: my friends, J. Bronson Case, of Kansas City, Missouri, Elizabeth E. Wellington, of Bronxville, New York, Louise Lawrence Meigs, wife of Ferris J. Meigs, of Bronxville, New York, and May Custer Elmer, wife of Charles Elmer, of 14 Clark Street, Brooklyn, New York, but this suggestion is not to be construed as in any way limiting the absoluteness of the discretion of my Executor with respect to such disposition and I direct that such discretion shall not be subject to review by any person or authority.

FIFTH: All the rest, residue and remainder of my property, both real and personal, wheresoever situated, of which I may die seized or possessed, or to which I may be entitled at the time of my decease, including the proceeds of the sale of any real property owned by me, I give, devise and bequeath to VASSAR COLLEGE, located at Poughkeepsie, New York, IN TRUST, to retain the principal thereof as a separate fund, and from time to time, in its discretion, to change the investment thereof and to invest and reinvest the same in securities of the same classes as those in which trustee by the law of the State of New York are authorized to invest trust funds; to collect the income therefrom, and to apply such income for the support and education of the daughters of commissioned officers in the regular army of the United States; preferable the assistance here provided shall be given to daughters of such officers who at the commencement of such assistance, may be located at distant stations outside of the continental United States. The assistance so to be rendered to said daughters may, in the discretion of the said College, be applied for support, education and instruction in schools preparatory to going to College, but it is my desire that it shall only assist those who intend to take a College course and who show a promise intellectually to be able to go on with the same. I have no purpose to assist girls who intend only to take a course in some preparatory school or institution other than a College and to stop their work in such other institution. It is my desire especially that such assistance shall be rendered to such daughters while in College. It may be extended to aid them in post-graduate work either in Vassar or some other institution, provided in the judgment of those administering this fund they will profit by such post-graduate work. In case there shall not be sufficient demand for the use of such fund for the daughters of army officers, as above provided, in the discretion of those having the administration of said fund, the same may be used for the education and assistance of other girls deemed worthy, but it is my desire that such employment of any part of the income from said fund for any year would not require that it should be continued for a succeeding year, to the exclusion of those who are intended to be the primary objects of my bounty. The said fund shall be known as the "GENERAL GEORGE ARMSTRONG CUSTER AND ELIZABETH BACON CUSTER SCHOLARSHIP FUND FOR DAUGHTERS OF ARMY OFFICERS." The ages of the girls who shall be entitled to participate in the benefit of said fund, whether in a preparatory school or otherwise, shall be entirely within the good judgment and discretion of those called upon to administer the fund, having in mind my desires as expressed above.

THE FOREGOING INSTRUMENT, consisting of five type-written pages, including this page, of which each page is signed by the Testatrix, was signed, sealed, published and declared by the above named Testatrix, ELIZABETH B. CUSTER, as and for her Last Will and Testament, in the presence of us, who, in her presence, at her request, and in the presence of each other, have hereunto subscribed our names as witnesses the day and year last above written, this Attestation Clause having first been read aloud.

Name William F. Gerlach   Residence 107-54 Robard Lane,

                                             Queens Village, N.Y.

Name Charles F. Wheaton   Residence 108 Valentine Lane

                                             Yonkers, N.Y.

Name Mansfield Ferry   Residence 62 East 92nd St.,

                                             Manhattan

NOTES

INTRODUCTION

1. Hunt, Frazier, *The Romantic Soldier* (Brooklyn, NY: Arrow & Trooper Publications, 1992), 41–42; Ladenheim, J. C., *Custer's Thorn: The Life of Frederick W. Benteen* (Westminster, MA: Heritage Books, 2007), 195; Yankton Press, May 31, 1877; Marcus, Reno, *The Official Record of a Court of Inquiry Convened at Chicago, Illinois,* January 13, 1879.

2. Ladenheim, *Custer's Thorn*, 95.

3. Ibid., 106; Letter to Theodore Goldin from Frederick Benteen, February 1896.

4. Benteen, Frederick, *Official Testimony of a Court Inquiry,* March 1879.

5. *The Dakotaian,* May 31, 1877; Russell, Jerry, *1876: Facts about Custer and the Battle of the Little Bighorn* (Cambridge, MA: Da Capo Press, 1999), 209.

CHAPTER 1: BEFORE GEORGE

1. "Life in the Barracks," *The Lowell Daily Sun,* January 31, 1894.

2. Ibid.

3. Ibid.

4. Ibid.

5. Elizabeth Custer Papers Collection: OGL #1496 (Elwyn B. Robinson Department of Special Collections, Chester Fritz Library, University of North Dakota), 33

6. Hammond, John L., Winfield S. Hancock, and George A. Custer, "Custer Against the Sioux Indians," *Journal of the American Academy,* Vol. XLVI 3; Leckie, Shirley, *Elizabeth Bacon Custer and the Making of a Myth* (Norman: University of Oklahoma Press, 1993), 15.

7. Merington, Marguerite, *The Custer Story: The Life and Intimate Letters of General George A. Custer and His Wife Elizabeth* (Lincoln: University of Nebraska Press, 1950), 47.

8. Arruda, Suzanne, "The Girl He Left Behind," *Journal of the American Academy,* Vol. XLVI, No. 3, 25.

9. Elizabeth Custer Papers Collection: OGL #1496, 22–35.

10. Elizabeth Bacon Custer's Journals, Western Americana Collection / Elizabeth Custer Manuscript Collection (The Beinecke Rare Book and Manuscript Library, Yale University), March 14, 1853, April 24, 1853.

11. Ibid., January, 5, 1854, January 25, 1854, February 22, 1854.

12. Ibid., August 27, 1854.

13. Ibid., February 1858; Wert, Jeffry, *Custer: The Controversial Life of George Armstrong Custer* (New York: Simon & Schuster, 1997).

14. Leckie, *Elizabeth Bacon Custer and the Making of a Myth,* 11–12.

15. Ibid., 12; Frost, Lawrence, *General Custer's Libbie* (Seattle, WA: Superior Publishing Company, 1976), 26–27.

16. Elizabeth Bacon Custer's Journals, January 2, 1856, January 3, 1856.

17. Merington, *The Custer Story,* 41.

18. Ibid., 43.

19. Ibid., 44–45.

20. Poolman, Jeremy, *A Wounded Thing Must Hide: In Search of Libbie Custer* (New York: Bloomsbury Press, 2002), 104.

21. Leighton, Margaret, *The Story of General Custer* (New York: Grosset & Dunlap, 1954), 89.

22. Merington, *The Custer Story*, 47.

23. Elizabeth Custer Papers Collection: OGL #1496, Letter from George to Elizabeth, November 24, 1863.

24. Ladenheim, *Custer's Thorn*, 69

Chapter 2: Courting Elizabeth

1. Frost, *General Custer's Libbie*, 51.

2. Ward, Geoffrey, Ric Burns, and Ken Burns, *The Civil War* (New York: Random House, 1994), 144; Leighton, *The Story of General Custer*, 65.

3. Ibid., 76–77.

4. Frost, *General Custer's Libbie*, 51.

5. Poolman, *A Wounded Thing Must Hide*, 102.

6. Letters from Elliot Bates to Elizabeth, July 1876, Western Americana Collection / Elizabeth Custer Manuscript Collection (The Beinecke Rare Book and Manuscript Library, Yale University); Merington, *The Custer Story*, 48.

7. Elizabeth Bacon Custer's Journals, October 19, 1862.

8. Merington, *The Custer Story*, 47.

9. Ibid., 3.

10. Ronsheim, Milton, *The Life of a General*, 3; Leighton, *The Story of General Custer*, 17.

11. Whittaker, Frederick, *A Complete Life of General George A. Custer* (New York: Sheldon & Company, 1876), 13.

12. Leighton, *The Story of General Custer*, 54.

13. Williams, Rick, West Point Library Files, *Custer's Academy Years at West Point*, West Point Library Files, West Point; Frost, Lawrence, *Custer's Album* (Norman: University of Oklahoma Press, 1990), 192.

14. Whittaker, *A Complete Life of General George A. Custer*, 94; Leighton, *The Story of General Custer*, 75.

15. Leighton, *The Story of General Custer*, 76–80; *Marysville Tribune*, Marysville, Ohio, July 24, 1861.

16. Leighton, *The Story of General Custer*, 78.

17. Whittaker, *A Complete Life of General George A. Custer*, 107–14.

18. Leighton, *The Story of General Custer*, 90.

19. Western Americana Collection / Elizabeth Custer Manuscript Collection (The Beinecke Rare Book and Manuscript Library, Yale University); Frost, *General Custer's Libbie*, 58.

20. Ibid.

21. Merington, *The Custer Story*, 50.

22. Western Americana Collection / Elizabeth Custer Manuscript Collection.

23. Recruiting poster dated January 1, 1864, from Tecumseh, Michigan; Frost, *General Custer's Libbie*, 55,

24. Dellenbaugh, Frederick, *George Armstrong Custer* (New York: Lumos Publishing, Inc., 2008), 22–34; Monaghan, Jay, *Custer: The Life of General George Armstrong Custer* (Lincoln: University of Nebraska Press, 1959), 133–35.

25. Ladenheim, J. C., *Custer's Thorn*, 93; Benteen, Frederick, *Cavalry Scraps: The Writings of Frederick W. Benteen* (East Stroudsburg, PA: Guidon Press, 1886), 17.

26. Merington, *The Custer Story*, 71.

27. Western Americana Collection / Elizabeth Custer Manuscript Collection.

28. Frost, *General Custer's Libbie*, 81.

29. Western Americana Collection / Elizabeth Custer Manuscript Collection.

30. Merington, *The Custer Story*, 75.

31. Ibid., 78–84.

32. Western Americana Collection / Elizabeth Custer Manuscript Collection.

33. Frost, *General Custer's Libbie*, 92–93.

34. Ibid.

CHAPTER 3: NEWLYWEDS

1. Frost, *General Custer's Libbie*, 96; Johnson, Dorothy M., *Some Went West* (Lincoln: University of Nebraska Press, 1997), 115–16; Leckie, *Elizabeth Bacon Custer and the Making of a Myth*, 36–37.

2. Western Americana Collection / Elizabeth Custer Manuscript Collection.

3. Ibid., June 1865; Frost, *General Custer's Libbie*, 97.

4. Ibid., 96.

5. Ibid.

6. Albright, Evan J., "Custer's Cape Cod Mistress," *Cape Cod Confidential* (Mystery Lane Press, 2005), 1–6.

7. Ibid.; Martin, Samuel J., *Union Captain Judson Kilpatrick* (Mechanicsburg, PA: Stackpole Books, 2002), 10.

8. Albright, "Custer's Cape Cod Mistress," 1–6.

9. Merington, *The Custer Story*, 84, Frost, *General Custer's Libbie*, 94

10. Ibid., 87.

11. Frost, *General Custer's Libbie*, 98.

12. Western Americana Collection / Elizabeth Custer Manuscript Collection.

13. Merington, *The Custer Story*, 90–91.

14. Ibid.

15. Katz, Mark, *Custer in Photographs* (Garryowen, MT: Custer Battlefield Museum Publishing, 2001), 44.

16. Merington, *The Custer Story*, 92–94.

17. Carroll, John M., *Camp Talk: The Very Private Letters of Frederick W. Benteen of the 7th U.S. Cavalry to His Wife, 1871 to 1888* (Mattituck, NY: J. M. Carroll & Company, 1983), xiii.

18. Ibid., xii.

19. Ladenheim, *Custer's Thorn*, 106; Barry, D. F., *Some D. F. Barry Correspondence* (Edited by Steve Fickert, Brooklyn, NY: Arrow & Trooper Publications, 1993), 25.

20. Merington, *The Custer Story*, 97–98.

21. Ward, *The Civil War*, 298, 366.

22. Sheridan, Philip, *Sheridan Memoirs: Personal Memoirs of Philip Sheridan, General, United States Army*, Vol. I (New York: Charles L. Webster Co., 1988), 374–75; Merington, *The Custer Story*, 97–98.

23. Monaghan, *Custer: The Life of General George Armstrong Custer*, 200.

24. *The Monroe Monitor*, June 15, 1864.

25. *New York Tribune*, August 20, 1864.

26. Merington, *The Custer Story*, 102.

27. Ibid., 99, 112.

28. Ibid., 116–18.

29. Western Americana Collection / Elizabeth Custer Manuscript Collection.

30. Merington, *The Custer Story*, 126–27.

31. Ibid., 109.

32. Ibid., 128.

33. Ibid., 131–32.

34. Ibid., 178–79.

35. Frost, *Custer's Album*, 61, 67.

36. Leighton, *The Story of General Custer*, 111.

CHAPTER 4: COMMON ENEMIES

1. Ladenheim, *Custer's Thorn*, 91.

2. Ibid., 93.

3. Ibid.

4. Ibid.

5. Ibid., 70–74.

6. Carroll, *Camp Talk*, xi–xx.

7. Katz, *Custer in Photographs*, 64–65.

8. Ward, *The Civil War*, 396.

9. Custer, Elizabeth, *Tenting on the Plains* (New York: Webster & Co., 1893), 18.

10. Leighton, *The Story of General Custer*, 114.

11. Utley, Robert M., *Cavalier in Buckskin: George Armstrong Custer and the Western Military Frontier* (Norman: University of Oklahoma Press, 2001), 38; Custer, *Tenting on the Plains*, 46.

12. Frost, *General Custer's Libbie*, 135.

13. Custer, *Tenting on the Plains*, 31.

14. Ibid., 47.

15. Frost, *General Custer's Libbie*, 137.

16. Custer, *Tenting on the Plains*, 53.

17. Ibid., 98.

18. Merington, *The Custer Story*, 174–75; Carroll, John M., *Custer's Cavalry Occupation of Hempstead & Austin, Texas* (Brooklyn, NY: Arrow & Trooper Publications, 2001), 17–20.

19. Custer, *Tenting on the Plains*, 75.

20. Ibid., 129; Frost, *General Custer's Libbie*, 140.

21. Merington, *The Custer Story*, 174–75.

22. Custer, *Tenting on the Plains*, 79.

23. Western Americana Collection / Elizabeth Custer Manuscript Collection.

24. Merington, *The Custer Story*, 175–79.

25. Frost, *General Custer's Libbie*, 171; Utley, *Cavalier in Buckskin*, 39; Barry, *Some, D. F. Barry Correspondence*, 23.

26. Western Americana Collection / Elizabeth Custer Manuscript Collection; Merington, *The Custer Story*, 159.

27. Carroll, *Custer's Cavalry Occupation of Hempstead & Austin, Texas*, 20–28.

28. Custer, *Tenting on the Plains*, 138.

29. Frost, *General Custer's Libbie*, 144.

30. Leckie, *Elizabeth Bacon Custer and the Making of a Myth*, 60–61.

31. Hatch, Thom, *The Custer Companion: A Comprehensive Guide to the Life of George Armstrong Custer and the Plains Indian Wars* (Mechanicsburg, PA: Stackpole Books, 2002), 67–68; Connell,

Evan, *Son of the Morning Star* (New York: North Point Press, 1997), 281–83; Utley, *Cavalier in Buckskin,* 107–8.

32. Cunningham, Michele, *Mexico and the Foreign Policy of Napoleon III* (Basingstoke, England: Palgrave Macmillan, 2001), 56–60; Merington, *The Custer Story,* 177.

33. Utley, *Cavalier in Buckskin,* 39; Leighton, *The Story of General Custer,* 115.

34. Western Americana Collection / Elizabeth Custer Manuscript Collection.

35. Ibid.

36. Leighton, *The Story of General Custer,* 116.

37. Merington, *The Custer Story,* 182.

38. Ibid., 183.

39. Custer, *Tenting on the Plains,* 208.

40. Ibid.; Western Americana Collection / Elizabeth Custer Manuscript Collection.

41. Custer, *Tenting on the Plains,* 212.

42. Ibid.

43. Western Americana Collection / Elizabeth Custer Manuscript Collection.

44. Frost, *General Custer's Libbie,* 157; Custer, *Tenting on the Plains,* 366.

45. Ibid., 367.

Chapter 5: Missing Elizabeth

1. Custer, *Tenting on the Plains,* 213, 380–85.

2. Ibid., 241; Frost, *General Custer's Libbie*, 158; Monaghan, *Custer: The Life of General George Armstrong Custer,* 281–83.

3. Custer, Elizabeth, "Mrs. Custer at Fort Riley," Edited by Minnie Dubbs, Millbrook, Kansas, Historical Quarterlies Spring 1974 Vol. 40, No. 1; Custer, Elizabeth, *Mrs. Custer on the Plains: Life in Kansas* (Brooklyn, NY: Arrow & Trooper Publications, 1993), 2–4.

4. Leckie, *Elizabeth Bacon Custer and the Making of a Myth,* 90–92.

5. Custer, *Tenting on the Plains,* 397; Frost, *General Custer's Libbie,* 159–60.

6. Ibid.

7. Utley, *Cavalier in Buckskin,* 47; Ladenheim, *Custer's Thorn,* 68–71.

8. Ibid.

9. Carroll, John M., *A Graphologist Looks at Custer and Some of His Friends (and a Few Enemies)* (Brooklyn, NY: Arrow & Trooper Publications, 1997), 7.

10. Frost, *General Custer's Libbie,* 158.

11. Custer, *Tenting on the Plains,* 453–55.

12. Ibid.

13. Leighton, *The Story of General Custer,* 122.

14. George Custer, *My Life on the Plains* (New York: Sheldon & Co., 1874), 39–47.

15. Custer, *Tenting on the Plains,* 484.

16. Ladenheim, *Custer's Thorn,* 71.

17. Barnett, Louise, *Touched by Fire: The Life, Death, & Mythic Afterlife of George Armstrong Custer* (New York: Henry Holt & Co., 1996), 197; Carroll, John M., *Benteen-Goldin Letters on Custer and His Last Battle* (Lincoln, University of Nebraska Press, 1991), 247.

18. Ibid.; Ladenheim, *Custer's Thorn*, 71.

19. Bowman, John S., *The American West Year by Year* (New York: Crescent Books, 1995), 94.

20. Custer, *Tenting on the Plains*, 485.

21. Leighton, *The Story of General Custer*, 124.

22. Ibid.

23. Custer, *My Life on the Plains*, 17.

24. Monaghan, *Custer: The Life of General George Armstrong Custer*, 284.

25. Utley, *Cavalier in Buckskin*, 49.

26. Custer, *Tenting on the Plains*, 490.

27. Ibid., 491.

28. Custer, *My Life on the Plains*, 270; Katz, *Custer in Photographs*, 149.

29. Merington, *The Custer Story*, 201.

30. Katz, *Custer in Photographs*, 140–42.

31. Monaghan, *Custer: The Life of General George Armstrong Custer*, 291.

32. Ladenheim, *Custer's Thorn*, 73.

33. Merington, *The Custer Story*, 205; Katz, *Custer in Photographs*, 149.

34. Ibid., 206.

35. Monaghan, *Custer: The Life of General George Armstrong Custer*, 292.

36. Custer, *Tenting on the Plains*, 596.

37. Merington, *The Custer Story*, 166.

38. Frost, *General Custer's Libbie*, 166–68.

39. Ladenheim, *Custer's Thorn*, 7–10, 70–74; Carroll, John M., *Custer in the Civil War: His Unfinished Memoirs* (San Rafael, CA: Presidio

Press, 1977); Leckie, *Elizabeth Bacon Custer and the Making of a Myth,* 102.

40. Utley, *Cavalier in Buckskin,* 41.

41. Custer, *Tenting on the Plains,* 354; Custer, *My Life on the Plains,* 77–79.

42. Frost, Lawrence, *The Court-Martial of General George Armstrong Custer* (Norman: University of Oklahoma Press, 1980), 41–42; Daubenmier, Judy, "Empty Saddles: Desertion from the Dashing U.S. Cavalry" (*Montana: The Magazine of the Western History,* Vol. 54, No. 3, October 1, 2004), 2–4.

43. Frost, *General Custer's Libbie,* 17; Leighton, *The Story of General Custer,* 34; Ladenheim, *Custer's Thorn,* 103.

44. Ibid., 103–4

45. Katz, *Custer in Photographs,* 140–42.

Chapter 6: Custer's Maiden

1. Frost, *General Custer's Libbie,* 175; Monaghan, *Custer: The Life of General George Armstrong Custer,* 303; Merington, *The Custer Story,* 216.

2. Ibid., 210; Frost, *The Court-Martial of General George Armstrong Custer,* 240–46.

3. *New York Times,* December 12, 1867.

4. Letter from George Custer to his cousin, Augusta, October 3, 1862, Western Americana Collection/George Custer Manuscript Collection (The Beinecke Rare Book and Manuscript Library, Yale University).

5. Leckie, *Elizabeth Bacon Custer and the Making of a Myth,* 103.

6. Utley, Robert M., ed., *Life in Custer's Cavalry: Diaries and Letters of Albert and Jennie Barnitz, 1867–1868* (Lincoln: University of Nebraska Press, 1987), 56–59.

7. Frost, *General Custer's Libbie*, 166–67; Custer, *Tenting on the Plains*, 632–49; Custer, *My Life on the Plains*, 48–50.

8. Western Americana Collection / Elizabeth Custer Manuscript Collection (The Beinecke Rare Book and Manuscript Library, Yale University).

9. Leighton, *The Story of General Custer*, 135; Custer, *Tenting on the Plains*, 341–342; Frost, *General Custer's Libbie*, 169.

10. Leighton, *The Story of General Custer*, 135.

11. Atherton, R. G., *William T. Sherman* (Memphis: Tennessee General Books, LLC, 1956), 213, 223; Monaghan, *Custer: The Life of General George Custer*, 304; Utter, Jack, *American Indians: Answers to Today's Questions* (Norman: University of Oklahoma Press, 2002), 53–54; Horsley, James, *Washita: Genocide on the Great Plains* (Washita Battlefield National Historic Site, Cheyenne, Oklahoma, 1994), 117–19.

12. U.S. Military telegram from General Philip Sheridan to the army, September 24, 1868, Western Americana Collection / George Custer Manuscript Collection (The Beinecke Rare Book and Manuscript Library, Yale University).

13. Chun, Clayton, *U.S. Army in the Plains Indian Wars 1865–91* (Essex, England: Osprey Publishing, 2004), 36–39.

14. Monaghan, *Custer: The Life of General George Armstrong Custer*, 305.

15. Leighton, *The Story of General Custer*, 136.

16. *Monroe Commercial Newspaper*, August 27, 1868.

17. Custer, Elizabeth, *Following the Guidon* (New York: Harper & Brothers, 1890), 12.

18. Utley, *Cavalier in Buckskin*, 59; Merington, *The Custer Story*, 216.

19. Custer, *Following the Guidon*, 11.

20. Ibid., 15–16.

21. Merington, *The Custer Story*, 219.

22. Letter to Elizabeth Custer from George Custer, October 26, 1868, Western Americana Collection / Elizabeth Custer Manuscript Collection (The Beinecke Rare Book and Manuscript Library, Yale University).

23. Letter to Elizabeth Custer from George Custer, October 28, 1868, Western Americana Collection / Elizabeth Custer Manuscript Collection (The Beinecke Rare Book and Manuscript Library, Yale University).

24. Custer, *Following the Guidon*, 5–7; Monaghan, *Custer: The Life of General George Armstrong Custer*, 314–15; Katz, *Custer in Photographs*, 150; General Custer's Report to General Sheridan, November 28, 1868, Western Americana Collection / George Custer Manuscript Collection (The Beinecke Rare Book and Manuscript Library, Yale University).

25. Letter to Elizabeth Custer from George Custer, December 19, 1868; General Custer's Report to General Sheridan, November 28, 1868, Western Americana Collection / Elizabeth Custer Manuscript Collection (The Beinecke Rare Book and Manuscript Library, Yale University).

26. Custer, *My Life on the Plains*, 168; Monaghan, *Custer: The Life of General George Armstrong Custer*, 318.

27. Monaghan, *Custer: The Life of General George Armstrong Custer*, 318.

28. Chatfield, Harry, "Custer's Secret Romance" (*Western Frontier*, Summer 1978); Koster, John, "Squaring Custer's Triangle" (*Wild West Magazine*, Vol. 22, No. 1, June 2009).

29. Kelly-Custer, Gail, *Princess Monahsetah: The Concealed Wife of General Custer* (Victoria, British Columbia: Trafford Publishing, 2007), 15–19.

30. Custer, *Following the Guidon*, 22.

31. Custer, *Following the Guidon*, 91; Chatfield, "Custer's Secret Romance."

32. Custer, *My Life on the Plains*, 172–76.

33. Chatfield, "Custer's Secret Romance."

34. Ladenheim, *Custer's Thorn*, 106.

35. Custer, *Following the Guidon*, 90.

36. Leighton, *The Story of General Custer*, 141–42; Chatfield, "Custer's Secret Romance."

37. Merington, *The Custer Story*, 224.

38. Ibid.

39. Chatfield, "Custer's Secret Romance."

40. Monaghan, *Custer: The Life of General George Armstrong Custer*, 329.

41. Merington, *The Custer Story*, 225.

42. Custer, *My Life on the Plains*, 164.

43. Monaghan, *Custer: The Life of General George Armstrong Custer*, 328–30.

44. Ladenheim, *Custer's Thorn*, 112; Chatfield, "Custer's Secret Romance"; Kelly-Custer, *Princess Monahsetah*, 37, 48–49.

45. Custer, *Following the Guidon*, 95–97.

46. Ibid.

47. Koster, "Squaring Custer's Triangle."

48. Chatfield, "Custer's Secret Romance."

49. Leckie, Shirley A., "Custer's Luck Runs Out" (*Montana: The Magazine of Western History* Vol. 43, No. 3, Summer 1993); Ladenheim, *Custer's Thorn*, 112.

50. Monaghan, *Custer: The Life of General George Armstrong Custer*, 331.

51. Custer, *Following the Guidon*, 71–72.

52. Monaghan, *Custer: The Life of General George Armstrong Custer*, 331–32.

53. Frost, *General Custer's Libbie*, 183–84; Custer, *Following the Guidon*, 153–54.

54. Monaghan, *Custer: The Life of General George Armstrong Custer*, 332; Carroll, John M., *Benteen-Goldin Letters on Custer and His Last Battle*, 258; Barry, *Some D. F. Barry Correspondence*, 27.

55. *Benteen-Goldin Letters on Custer and His Last Battle* (Lincoln: University of Nebraska Press, 1991), 258_59.

CHAPTER 7: TROUBLE APART

1. "Centennial Scrapbook," *The Register*, Danville, Virginia, April 7, 1968.

2. Merington, *The Custer Story*, 231.

3. Monaghan, *Custer: The Life of General George Armstrong Custer*, 332.

4. *New York Times*, November 22, 1869.

5. Letter from George Custer to Elizabeth Custer, December 2, 1869, Western Americana Collection / Elizabeth Custer Manuscript Collection (The Beinecke Rare Book and Manuscript Library, Yale University).

6. Merington, *The Custer Story*, 231.

7. Marquis, Thomas B., *She Watched Custer's Last Battle / Which Indian Killed Custer / Custer Soldiers Not Buried* (Brooklyn, NY:

Arrow & Trooper Publications, 1992), 3; Barry, *Some D. F. Barry Correspondence*, 24.

8. Merington, *The Custer Story*, 231.

9. *Thomas Weir Military Records & Personal Letters 1863–1876* (National Archives and Records Administration, M1064C:492).

10. Katz, *Custer in Photographs*, 144–45; Bingham, Anne, "Wild Life on the Plains" (*Kansas Historical Quarterlies*, Vol. XV, Summer 1972), 501–3

11. Ibid., 504–6.

12. Leighton, *The Story of General Custer*, 160.

13. Merington, *The Custer Story*, 232.

14. Frost, *General Custer's Libbie*, 194.

15. *The Anglo-American Times*, November 30, 1867.

16. Sherwood, Glenn, *A Labor of Love: The Art of Vinnie Ream* (New York: Sunshine Press Publications, 1997), 103–4.

17. Letter from George Custer to Elizabeth Custer, July 1871, Western Americana Collection / Elizabeth Custer Manuscript Collection (The Beinecke Rare Book and Manuscript Library, Yale University); Merington, *The Custer Story*, 233.

18. Frost, *General Custer's Libbie*, 191; Ladenheim, *Custer's Thorn*, 122–24.

19. Leckie, "Custer's Luck Runs Out."

20. Frost, *General Custer's Libbie*, 195.

21. Letter from George Custer to Elizabeth Custer, May 8, 1871, Western Americana Collection / Elizabeth Custer Manuscript Collection (The Beinecke Rare Book and Manuscript Library, Yale University); Merington, *The Custer Story*, 232–33.

22. Frost, *General Custer's Libbie*, 193.

23. Merington, *The Custer Story*, 238.

24. Frost, *General Custer's Libbie*, 192.

25. Merington, *The Custer Story*, 238.

26. Ibid.

27. Letter from George Custer to his mother, September 20, 1871, Western Americana Collection / George Custer Manuscript Collection (The Beinecke Rare Book and Manuscript Library, Yale University); Frost, *General Custer's Libbie*, 197.

28. Ibid.

29. Letter from George Custer to Elizabeth Custer, February 9, 1872, Western Americana Collection / George Custer Manuscript Collection (The Beinecke Rare Book and Manuscript Library, Yale University).

30. Monaghan, *Custer: The Life of General George Armstrong Custer*, 338.

31. Merington, *The Custer Story*, 241.

32. Frost, *General Custer's Libbie*, 198.

33. Ladenheim, *Custer's Thorn*, 122–24.

34. Monaghan, *Custer: The Life of General George Armstrong Custer*, 336; Merington, *The Custer Story*, 246.

35. *The New York Herald,* February 28, 1872; *The Cambridge Jeffersonian,* February 1, 1872.

36. Elizabeth Bacon Custer's Journals, February 1872.

37. Custer, George, Letter to John M. Buckley, June 4, 1872 (Burton Historical Collection, Detroit Public Library, Detroit, Michigan).

38. Custer, Elizabeth, *Boots and Saddles* (New York: Harper & Brothers, 1885), 13.

39. Monaghan, *Custer: The Life of General George Armstrong Custer*, 339.

40. Custer, *Boots and Saddles*, 10.

41. Ibid., 11.

42. Ibid., 15.

43. Ibid., 16; Monaghan, *Custer: The Life of General George Armstrong Custer*, 340; Merington, *The Custer Story*, 251.

Chapter 8: Plains Living

1. Frost, *General Custer's Libbie*, 185.

2. Ladenheim, *Custer's Thorn*, 135.

3. Ibid., 162.

4. Katz, *Custer in Photographs*, 151–52; David Sloane Stanley (www.wikipedia.org); Monaghan, *Custer: The Life of General George Armstrong Custer*, 340.

5. Custer, *Boots and Saddles*, 26–35; Frost, *General Custer's Libbie*, 202–3; Katz, *Custer in Photographs*, 151–52.

6. Custer, Elizabeth, Letter to Mr. Fox, October 4, 1927 (South Dakota Historical Society); Custer, *Boots and Saddles*, 28, 31–34.

7. Custer, *Boots and Saddles*, 28, 31–34.

8. Ibid., 46.

9. Frost, *General Custer's Libbie*, 204.

10. Custer, *Boots and Saddles*, 60.

11. Ibid., 64.

12. Ibid., 67.

13. Ibid., 69.

14. Merington, *The Custer Story*, 248; Monaghan, *Custer: The Life of General George Armstrong Custer*, 340–41; Frost, *General Custer's Libbie*, 204–5.

15. Custer, *Boots and Saddles*, 70–71.

16. Ladenheim, *Custer's Thorn*, 130–31; Monaghan, *Custer: The Life of General George Armstrong Custer*, 341.

17. Ibid., 341–42.

18. Ibid., 343; Merington, *The Custer Story*, 251; Barry, *Some D. F. Barry Correspondence*, 12.

19. Barry, *Some D. F. Barry Correspondence*, 12;.Frost, *General Custer's Libbie*, 204–5.

20. Monaghan, *Custer: The Life of General George Armstrong Custer*, 350–51; Merington, *The Custer Story*, 251–53, 265.

21. Merington, *The Custer Story*, 253–54; Utley, *Cavalier in Buckskin*, 118–19.

22. Utley, *Cavalier in Buckskin*, 118–19.

23. Ibid., 119; Ladenheim, *Custer's Thorn*, 132.

24. *New York Times*, July 17, 1873; "The Yellowstone Expedition," *New York Times*, September 10, 1873.

25. Forman, John F., "Custer's Greatest Blunder," *Real West Magazine*, Vol. VIII, No. 43, September 1965, 26–27.

26. Merington, *The Custer Story*, 252–53.

27. Utley, *Cavalier in Buckskin*, 125; Monaghan, *Custer: The Life of General George Armstrong Custer*, 351.

28. Custer, *Boots and Saddles*, 78.

29. Frost, *General Custer's Libbie*, 206.

30. Custer, *Boots and Saddles*, 80–81.

31. Ladenheim, *Custer's Thorn*, 137–38; Fougera, Katherine G., *With Custer's Cavalry* (New York: Iyer Press, 2007), 246.

32. Custer, *Boots and Saddles*, 138–39; Frost, *General Custer's Libbie*, 208.

33. Frost, *General Custer's Libbie,* 211; Monaghan, *Custer: The Life of General George Armstrong Custer,* 353.

34. Katz, *Custer in Photographs,* 150; Merington, *The Custer Story,* 273.

35. Western Americana Collection / Elizabeth Custer Manuscript Collection.

36. Frost, *General Custer's Libbie,* 212.

37. Custer, *Boots and Saddles,* 133.

38. Merington, *The Custer Story,* 272–73.

39. Ibid.; Ward, Geoffrey, *The Civil War,* 292–93.

40. Custer, *Boots and Saddles,* 158–59.

41. Ladenheim, *Custer's Thorn,* 141, 290.

42. *Monroe Commercial Newspaper,* November 5, 1874; Frost, *General Custer's Libbie,* 214.

43. Western Americana Collection / Elizabeth Custer Manuscript Collection, September 23, 1873.

44. Custer, *Boots and Saddles,* 192.

45. *New York Herald,* February 28, 1875.

46. Custer, *Boots and Saddles,* 187, 192–93.

47. Forman, "Custer's Greatest Blunder," 26–27.

48. Frost, *General Custer's Libbie,* 216; Monaghan, *Custer: The Life of General George Armstrong Custer,* 360.

49. Monaghan, *Custer: The Life of General George Armstrong Custer,* 360.

50. Custer, *Boots and Saddles,* 181.

51. Katz, *Custer in Photographs,* 146.

52. Monaghan, *Custer: General George Armstrong Custer,* 361.

53. Hunt, *The Romantic Soldier,* 25.

54. Frost, *General Custer's Libbie*, 217; Monaghan, *Custer: General George Armstrong Custer*, 363.

55. Hunt, *The Romantic Soldier*, 26.

56. Custer, *Boots and Saddles*, 149.

CHAPTER 9: LOSING GEORGE

1. Monaghan, *Custer: The Life of General George Armstrong Custer*, 392.

2. Leighton, *The Story of General Custer*, 164–65.

3. Ibid.; Merington, *The Custer Story*, 297–98; Frost, *General Custer's Libbie*, 226; Custer, *Boots and Saddles*, 216–17.

4. Custer, *Boots and Saddles*, 222.

5. Leckie, *Elizabeth Bacon Custer and the Making of a Myth*, 190; *The Billings Gazette*, May 27, 1961; Fougera, *With Custer's Cavalry*, 263.

6. Fougera, *With Custer's Cavalry*, 264–65; Custer, *Boots and Saddles*, 222–24.

7. Custer, *Boots and Saddles*, 263; Andrews, Elisha B., *The History of the Last Quarter Century in the U.S.*, Vol. 1 (New York: General Books, LLC, 2009), 186; Frost, *General Custer's Libbie*, 227.

8. Frost, *General Custer's Libbie*, 227.

9. Custer, *Boots and Saddles*, 11–12.

10. Frost, *General Custer's Libbie*, 218–19.

11. Custer, *Boots and Saddles*, 215.

12. Merington, *The Custer Story*, 277.

13. Frost, *General Custer's Libbie*, 219.

14. Merington, *The Custer Story*, 279–80; Frost, *Custer's Album*, 148.

15. Monaghan, *Custer: The Life of General George Armstrong Custer*, 364–65.

16. *The Indiana Democrat*, April 6, 1876. "Belknap and Grant."

17. Custer, *My Life on the Plains*, 103.

18. Ladenheim, *Custer's Thorn*, 151; Monaghan, *Custer: The Life of George Armstrong Custer*, 363; Frost, *General Custer's Libbie*, 220.

19. Frost, *General Custer's Libbie*, 270; Merington, *The Custer Story*, 281–82.

20. Merington, *The Custer Story*, 283.

21. *New York Herald*, March 31, 1876; Monaghan, *Custer: The Life of General George Armstrong Custer*, 366.

22. *Thomas Weir Military Records & Personal Letters 1863–1876*; Frost, *General Custer's Libbie*, 171.

23. Monaghan, *Custer: The Life of General George Armstrong Custer*, 366–67; Frost, *General Custer's Libbie*, 221–22.

24. *The Indiana Democrat*, April 6, 1876. "Belknap and Grant."

25. Letter from William Belknap to General Alfred Terry, April 13, 1876. Elizabeth Custer Collection (Elizabeth Custer Library & Museum, Garryowen, Montana).

26. *The Anglo-American Times*, April 21, 1876; William W. Belknap (www.wikipedia.org); Merington, *The Custer Story*, 294–95.

27. Merington, *The Custer Story*, 285.

28. Ibid., 289; Frost, *General Custer's Libbie*, 223; Western Americana Collection / Elizabeth Custer Manuscript Collection.

29. Frost, *General Custer's Libbie*, 223.

30. Hunt, *The Romantic Soldier*, 27.

31. Ibid., 28; *The Anglo-American Times*, May 19, 1876.

32. Hunt, *The Romantic Soldier*, 28; Western Americana Collection / Elizabeth Custer Manuscript Collection.

33. *Monroe Evening News*, April 7, 1933.

34. Ibid.

35. Frost, *General Custer's Libbie*, 226; Custer, *Boots and Saddles*, 216.

36. Custer, *Boots and Saddles*, 219.

37. Ibid., 216–18.

38. Leighton, *The Story of General Custer*, 164–65.

39. Custer, *Boots and Saddles*, 220–21; Donovan, Jim, *Custer and the Little Bighorn* (Stillwater, MN: Voyageur Press, 2001), 136.

40. Leighton, *The Story of General Custer*, 300.

41. Frost, *General Custer's Libbie*, 227; Custer, *Boots and Saddles*, 222; *Billings Gazette*, May 27, 1961.

42. Custer, *Boots and Saddles*, 220–21; Donovan, *Custer and the Little Bighorn*, 136.

CHAPTER 10: SUDDENLY ALONE

1. *Frontier Fighters*, Episode 24, June 8, 1926 (Western Historical Manuscript Collection SL256, University of Missouri, St. Louis).

2. Custer, *Boots and Saddles*, 222.

3. Ibid., 224; Russell, *1876: Facts about Custer and the Battle of the Little Bighorn*, 112–13; Donovan, *Custer and the Little Bighorn*, 142, 148–49.

4. Donovan, *Custer and the Little Bighorn*, 167; Monaghan, *Custer: The Life of General George Armstrong Custer*, 388.

5. Leighton, *The Story of General Custer*, 320.

6. "General Custer's Terrible Defeat," *Bethlehem Daily Times*, July 7, 1876.

7. Donovan, *Custer and the Little Bighorn*, 213–15.

8. Merington, *The Custer Story*, 321, 325.

9. Ibid., 323–24.

10. "Yellowstone Expedition," *New York Times*, September 9, 1876.

11. Marquis, *She Watched Custer's Last Battle / Which Indian Killed Custer / Custer Soldiers Not Buried*, 6–10.

12. Frost, *General Custer's Libbie*, 227; Merington, *The Custer Story*, 323.

13. Monaghan, *Custer: The Life of General George Armstrong Custer*, 392.

14. Donovan, *Custer and the Little Bighorn*, 194.

15. Forsyth, G. A., *The Story of the Soldier* (New York: D. Appleton & Company, 1900), 328.

16. McClellan, George B., *McClellan's Own Story* (London, England: Sampson Low, Marston, Searle, & Riverton, 1887), 365.

17. *Thomas Weir Military Records & Personal Letters 1863–1876*.

18. Donovan, *Custer and the Little Bighorn*, 184–86.

19. *Burlington Hawk-Eye*, August 24, 1876; *Monroe Commercial Newspaper*, August 17, 1876.

20. *Congressional Record* (44th Congress, 1st Session, Nos. 4627, 4628, 4629); *The Constitution*, July 16, 1876; Frost, *General Custer's Libbie*, 228.

21. Frost, *General Custer's Libbie*, 233.

22. Letter from Nellie Wadsworth to George Custer, Elizabeth Custer Collection (Elizabeth Custer Library & Museum, Garryowen, Montana).

23. Ibid.

24. Ladenheim, *Custer's Thorn*, 198; Frost, *General Custer's Libbie*, 238–39.

25. Elizabeth Custer Collection (Elizabeth Custer Library & Museum, Garryowen, Montana).

26. Kennedy, John B. "A Soldier's Widow" (*Collier's Weekly Magazine*, January 29, 1927), 10.

27. *New York Times*, July 9, 1876.

28. Merington, *The Custer Story*, 308.

29. Leckie, *Elizabeth Bacon Custer and the Making of a Myth*, 216–17; United States Sanitary Commission (www.wikipedia.org).

30. Donovan, *Custer and the Little Bighorn*, 201.

31. Elizabeth Custer Collection (Elizabeth Custer Library & Museum, Garryowen, Montana).

32. Letter to Elizabeth Custer from Elliot Bates, July 6, 1876, Elizabeth Custer Collection (Elizabeth Custer Library & Museum, Garryowen, Montana).

33. *Thomas Weir Military Records & Personal Letters 1863–1876.*

34. Frost, *General Custer's Libbie*, 237.

35. Ibid., 236; Whittaker, Frederick, "Custer Eulogy" (*Galaxy Magazine*, September 1876).

36. Donovan, Terrence J., *Brazen Trumpet: Frederick W. Benteen and the Battle of the Little Bighorn* (Bullhead City, AZ: Mohave West, 2009), 195.

37. *Thomas Weir Military Records & Personal Letters 1863–1876.*

38. Ibid.; Frost, *General Custer's Libbie*, 236; Whittaker, *A Complete Life of George A. Custer*, 183; Ladenheim, *Custer's Thorn*, 207.

39. Ladenheim, *Custer's Thorn*, 208.

40. Monaghan, *Custer: The Life of General George Armstrong Custer*, 398–99.

41. Barry, *Some D. F. Barry Correspondence*, 29.

42. Frost, *General Custer's Libbie*, 399.

43. Ibid., 249.

44. Hoagland, Loretta, *Lawrence Park: Bronxville's Turn-of-the-Century Art Colony* (New York: Lawrence Park Hilltop Association, Inc., 1992), 66–68.

45. Letter from Buffalo Bill Cody to Elizabeth Custer, August 13, 1886; Elizabeth Custer Collection (Elizabeth Custer Library & Museum, Garryowen, Montana); Frost, *General Custer's Libbie*, 250–53.

46. Frost, *General Custer's Libbie*, 266–67.

47. Elizabeth Custer Collection (Elizabeth Custer Library & Museum, Garryowen, Montana).

48. *New York Times*, June 25, 1931.

49. *Salt Lake Tribune*, April 16, 1933.

50. *San Antonio Express*, April 11, 1933.

51. *Billings Gazette*, April 5, 1933.

52. *Atlanta Journal*, May 24, 1897; Ladenheim, *Custer's Thorn*, 269.

53. *Salt Lake Tribune*, May 12, 1933.

54. *New York Herald*, June 25, 1926.

BIBLIOGRAPHY

BOOKS

Andrews, Elisha B. *The History of the Last Quarter Century in the U.S.*, Vol. 1. New York: General Books, LLC, 2009.

Atherton, R. G. *William T. Sherman*. Memphis: Tennessee General Books, LLC, 1956.

Barnett, Louise. *Touched by Fire: The Life, Death, & Mythic Afterlife of George Armstrong Custer*. New York: Henry Holt & Co., 1996.

Barry, D. F. *Some D. F. Barry Correspondence*. Edited by Steve Fickert. Brooklyn, NY: Arrow & Trooper Publications, 1993.

Benteen, Frederick. *Cavalry Scraps: The Writings of Frederick W. Benteen*. East Stroudsburg, PA: Guidon Press, 1886.

Benteen, Frederick. *Official Testimony of a Court Inquiry*, March 1879.

Bowman, John S. *The American West Year by Year*. New York: Crescent Books, 1995.

Brininstool, E. A. *The Custer Fight*. Hollywood, CA: Privately published by E. A. Brininstool, 1933.

Carroll, John M. *Benteen-Goldin Letters on Custer and His Last Battle*. Lincoln: University of Nebraska Press, 1991.

———. *Camp Talk: The Very Private Letters of Frederick W. Benteen of the 7th U.S. Cavalry to His Wife, 1871 to 1888*. Mattituck, NY: J. M. Carroll & Company, 1983.

———*Custer in the Civil War: His Unfinished Memoir.* San Rafael, CA: Presidio Press, 1977.

———. *Custer's Cavalry Occupation of Hempstead & Austin, Texas.* Brooklyn, NY: Arrow & Trooper Publications, 2001.

———. *General Custer and New Rumley, Ohio.* Brooklyn, NY: Arrow & Trooper Publications, 2001.

———. *A Graphologist Looks at Custer and Some of His Friends (and a Few Enemies).* Brooklyn, NY: Arrow & Trooper Publications, 1997.

Chun, Clayton. *U.S. Army in the Plains Indian Wars 1865–91.* Essex, England: Osprey Publishing, 2004.

Connell, Evan. *Son of the Morning Star.* New York: North Point Press, 1997.

Cunningham, Michele. *Mexico and the Foreign Policy of Napoleon III.* Basingstoke, England: Palgrave Macmillan, 2001.

Custer, Boston. *Letters from Boston Custer.* Edited by Tom O'Neil. Brooklyn, NY: Arrow & Trooper Publications, 1993.

Custer, Elizabeth. *Boots and Saddles.* New York: Harper & Brothers, 1885.

———. *Following the Guidon.* New York: Harper & Brothers, 1890.

———. *Libbie's Civil War.* Edited by Steve Fickert. Brooklyn, NY: Arrow & Trooper Publications, 2000.

———. *Libbie's Forgotten Scrapbook.* Compiled by Tom O'Neil. Brooklyn, NY: Arrow & Trooper Publications, 1991.

———. *Mrs. Custer on the Plains: Life in Kansas.* Brooklyn, NY: Arrow & Trooper Publications, 1993.

———. *Tenting on the Plains.* New York: Webster & Co., 1893.

Custer, Elizabeth, and George Custer. *Some Custer Letters.* Edited by Tom O'Neil. Brooklyn, NY: Arrow & Trooper Publications, 1993.

Custer, George. *My Life on the Plains.* New York: Sheldon & Co., 1874.

Dellenbaugh, Frederick S. *George Armstrong Custer.* New York: Lumos Publishing, Inc., 2008.

Dippie, Brian W. *Custer's Last Stand: The Anatomy of an American Myth.* Lincoln: University of Nebraska Press, 1994.

Donovan, Jim. *Custer and the Little Bighorn.* Stillwater, MN: Voyageur Press, 2001.

Donovan, Terrence. *Brazen Trumpet: Frederick W. Benteen and the Battle of the Little Bighorn.* Bullhead City, AZ: Mohave West, 2009.

Dustin, Fred. *George Armstrong Custer's Trial: The Aftermath,* Volume 1. Westerners Publications Limited. London, England, 2004.

Eales, Anne Bruner. *Army Wives on the American Frontier: Living by the Bugles.* Boulder, CO: Johnson Books, 1996.

Forsyth, G. A. *The Story of the Soldier.* New York: D. Appleton & Company, 1900.

Fougera, Katherine G. *With Custer's Cavalry.* New York: Iyer Press, 2007.

Frost, Lawrence. *The Court-Martial of General George Armstrong Custer.* Norman: University of Oklahoma Press, 1980.

———. *Custer's Album.* Norman: University of Oklahoma Press, 1990.

———. *General Custer's Libbie.* Seattle, WA: Superior Publishing Company, 1976.

Gänzl, Kurt. *Lydia Thompson: Queen of Burlesque.* New York & London: Routledge Press, 2002.

Hatch, Thom. *The Custer Companion: A Comprehensive Guide to the Life of George Armstrong Custer and the Plains Indian Wars.* Mechanicsburg, PA: Stackpole Books, 2002.

Hoagland, Loretta. *Lawrence Park: Bronxville's Turn-of-the-Century Art Colony.* New York: Lawrence Park Hilltop Association, Inc., 1992.

Hofling, Charles. *Custer and the Little Big Horn.* Detroit, MI: Wayne State University Press, 1981.

Horsley, James. *Washita: Genocide on the Great Plains.* Washita Battlefield National Historic Site. Cheyenne, Oklahoma, 1994.

Hunt, Frazier. *The Romantic Soldier.* Brooklyn, NY: Arrow & Trooper Publications, 1992.

Hutton, Paul, and Robert M. Utley. *The Custer Reader.* Norman: University of Oklahoma, 2004.

Johnson, Dorothy M. *Some Went West.* Lincoln: University of Nebraska Press, 1997.

Katz, Mark D. *Custer in Photographs.* Garryowen, MT: Custer Battlefield Museum Publishing, 2001.

Kelly-Custer, Gail. *Princess Monahsetah: The Concealed Wife of General Custer.* Victoria, British Columbia: Trafford Publishing, 2007.

Ladenheim, J. C. *Custer's Thorn: The Life of Frederick W. Benteen.* Westminster, MA: Heritage Books, 2007.

Leckie, Shirley. *Elizabeth Bacon Custer and the Making of a Myth.* Norman: University of Oklahoma Press, 1993.

Leighton, Margaret. *The Story of General Custer.* New York: Grosset & Dunlap, 1954.

Marquis, Thomas B. *She Watched Custer's Last Battle / Which Indian Killed Custer / Custer Soldiers Not Buried*. Brooklyn, NY: Arrow & Trooper Publications, 1992.

Martin, Samuel J. *Union Captain Judson Kilpatrick*. Mechanicsburg, PA: Stackpole Books, 2002.

McClellan, George B. *McClellan's Own Story*. London, England: Sampson Low, Marston, Searle, & Riverton, 1887.

McKale, William, and William D. Young. *Fort Riley: Citadel of the Frontier West*. Topeka: Kansas State Historical Society, 2003.

Merington, Marguerite. *The Custer Story: The Life and Intimate Letters of General George A. Custer and His Wife Elizabeth*. Lincoln: University of Nebraska Press, 1950.

Monaghan, Jay. *Custer: The Life of General George Armstrong Custer*. Lincoln: University of Nebraska Press, 1959.

Poolman, Jeremy. *A Wounded Thing Must Hide: In Search of Libbie Custer*. New York: Bloomsbury Press, 2002.

Robinson, Doane A. M. *A Brief History of South Dakota*. New York, Cincinnati, Chicago: American Book Company, 1905.

Russell, Jerry. *1876: Facts about Custer and the Battle of the Little Bighorn*. Cambridge, MA: Da Capo Press, 1999.

Sheridan, Philip. *Sheridan Memoirs: Personal Memoirs of Philip Sheridan, General, United States Army, Vol. I and II*. New York: Charles L. Webster Co., 1888.

Sherman, William T. *Memoirs of William Tecumseh Sherman*. New York: Da Capo Press, 1984.

Sherwood, Glenn. *A Labor of Love: The Art of Vinnie Ream*. New York: Sunshine Press Publications, 1997.

Utley, Robert M. *Cavalier in Buckskin: George Armstrong Custer and the Western Military Frontier.* Norman: University of Oklahoma Press, 2001.

Utley, Robert M., ed. *Life in Custer's Cavalry: Diaries and Letters of Albert and Jennie Barnitz, 1867–1868.* Lincoln: University of Nebraska Press, 1987.

Utter, Jack. *American Indians: Answers to Today's Questions.* Norman: University of Oklahoma Press, 2002.

Ward, Geoffrey C., Ric Burns, and Ken Burns. *The Civil War.* New York: Random House, 1994.

———. *The West: An Illustrated History.* New York: Little, Brown & Co., 1996.

Warner, Ezra J. *Generals in Blue: Lives of the Union Commanders.* Baton Rouge: Louisiana State University Press, 1964.

Watson, Elmo, and Don Russell. Edited by Steve Fickert. *Washita Massacre or Victory: Debating Cheyenne Accounts of the Battle.* Brooklyn, NY: Arrow & Trooper Publications, 1999.

Welsh, Jack D. *Medical Histories of Union Generals.* Kent, OH: Kent State University Press, 2005.

Wert, Jeffry. *Custer: The Controversial Life of George Armstrong Custer.* New York: Simon & Schuster, 1997.

Whittaker, Frederick. *A Complete Life of George A. Custer.* New York: Sheldon & Company, 1876.

MAGAZINES

Albright, Evan J. "Custer's Cape Cod Mistress." *Cape Cod Confidential.* Mystery Lane Press, 2005.

Arruda, Suzanne. "The Girl He Left Behind." *Journal of the American Academy*, Vol. XLVI, No. 3.

Bingham, Anne. "Wild Life on the Plains." *Kansas Historical Quarterlies*, Vol. XV, Summer 1972.

Chatfield, Harry. "Custer's Secret Romance." *Western Frontier*, Summer 1978.

Custer, Elizabeth. "Mrs. Custer at Fort Riley." Edited by Minnie Dubbs Millbrook. *Kansas Historical Quarterlies*, Spring 1974, Vol. 40, No. 1.

Daubenmier, Judy. "Empty Saddles: Desertion from the Dashing U.S. Cavalry." *Montana: The Magazine of Western History*, Vol. 54, No. 3, October 1, 2004.

Forman, John F. "Custer's Greatest Blunder." *Real West Magazine*, Vol. VIII, No. 43, September 1965.

Guziak, Margaret. "Army Informs Mrs. Custer of Husband's Death at the Little Bighorn." *Chronicle of the Old West*, Vol. 7, No. 8, July 2007.

Hammond, John L., Winfield S. Hancock, and George A. Custer. "Custer Against the Sioux Indians." *Journal of the American Academy*, Vol. XLVI 3.

Kennedy, John B. "A Soldier's Widow." *Collier's Weekly Magazine*, January 29, 1927.

Koster, John. "Squaring Custer's Triangle." *Wild West Magazine*, Vol. 22, No. 1, June 2009.

Leckie, Shirley. A. "Custer's Luck Runs Out." *Montana: The Magazine of Western History*, Vol. 43, No. 3, Summer 1993.

Michno, Gregory. "10 Myths of the Little Bighorn." *Wild West Magazine*, Vol. 21, No. 1, June 2008.

Milbrook, Minnie D. *Kansas Historical Quarterlies*, Vol. 36, No. 2, Summer 1970.

———. *Kansas Historical Quarterlies*, Vol. 40, No. 1, Spring 1974.

Shoemaker, Colonel John O. "The Custer Court-Martial." Fort Leavenworth Historical Society, Fort Leavenworth, KS. October 1971.

Sklenar, Larry. "Theodore W. Goldin: Little Bighorn Survivor and the Winner of the Medal of Honor." *The Wisconsin Magazine of History*, Vol. 80, No. 2, Winter 1996–97.

Smith, Robert B. "Benteen: Between a Rock and a Hard Place." *Wild West Magazine*, Vol. 23, No. 1, June 2010.

Whittaker, Frederick. "Custer Eulogy." *Galaxy Magazine*, September 1876.

NEWSPAPERS

"Theatricals and Amusements," *The Anglo-American Times*, London, England, November 30, 1867.

The Anglo-American Times, London, England, May 2, 1874.

The Anglo-American Times, London, England, April 21, 1876.

The Anglo-American Times, London, England, May 19, 1876.

The Atlanta Journal, May 24, 1897.

"General Custer's Terrible Defeat," *Bethlehem Daily Times*, Bethlehem, Pennsylvania, July 7, 1876.

The Billings Gazette, April 5, 1933.

The Billings Gazette, May 27, 1961.

The Billings Gazette, June 23, 1976.

"Custer's Raid," *The Bismarck Tribune,* May 13, 1874.

"The Indian War," *The Boston Daily Globe,* July 8, 1876.

Burlington Hawk-Eye, Burlington, Iowa, August 24, 1876.

The Cambridge Jeffersonian, Cambridge, Massachusetts, February 1, 1872.

"The Savage Sioux," *The Constitution,* Atlanta, Georgia, July 16, 1876.

The Dakotaian, May 31, 1877.

"About the Sioux War," *The Galveston Daily News,* July 16, 1876.

"Indian War Tidings," *The Galveston Daily News,* July 29, 1876.

"Belknap and Grant," *The Indiana Democrat,* Indiana, Pennsylvania, April 6, 1876.

The Indiana Progress, Indiana, Pennsylvania, July 26, 1877.

"Life in the Barracks," *The Lowell Daily Sun,* January 31, 1894.

Marysville Tribune, Marysville, Ohio, July 24, 1861.

Monroe Commercial Newspaper, August 27, 1868.

Monroe Commercial Newspaper, August 17, 1876.

Monroe Evening News, April 7, 1933.

The Monroe Monitor, June 15, 1864.

"Echoes from the Distant Past," O'Malley, M.G., *Montana Standard,* Butte, Montana, September 18, 1938.

The New York Herald, February 28, 1872.

The New York Herald, March 31, 1876.

The New York Herald, June 25, 1926.

"General George Custer," *The New York Times,* December 31, 1867.

The New York Times, November 22, 1869.

"The Yellowstone Expedition," *The New York Times,* July 17, 1873.

The New York Times, September 10, 1873.

"General Custer's Last Fight," *The New York Times,* July 5, 1876.

The New York Times, July 9, 1876.

"The Yellowstone Expedition," *The New York Times,* September 9, 1876.

The New York Times, May 28, 1882.

The New York Times, June 8, 1882.

The New York Times, December 10, 1904.

The New York Times, June 25, 1931.

The New York Tribune, August 20, 1864.

"Thundering Northwest," *The Oregon Standard Examiner,* September 3, 1933.

The Pall Mall Gazette, London, England, May 3, 1899.

"Centennial Scrapbook," *The Register,* Danville, Virginia, April 7, 1968.

Salt Lake Tribune, April 16, 1933.

Salt Lake Tribune, May 12, 1933.

The San Antonio Express, April 11, 1933.

WEBSITES
Battle of the Little Bighorn, www.wikipedia.org

Custer's Academy Years at West Point, www.angelfire.com/oh5/custer /Westpoint.html

Bibliography

David Sloane Stanley, www.wikipedia.org

Elizabeth Bacon Custer, www.ancestry.com

Thomas Weir, www.ohiohistory.org

United States Sanitary Commission, www.wikipedia.org

William W. Belknap, www.wikipedia.org

AUTHOR INTERVIEWS AND CORRESPONDENCE
Henry, Nadya (former director of Little Bighorn Battlefield
Monument). Telephone interview, August 24, 2009.

Kelly-Custer, Gail (author of *Princess Monahsetah: The Concealed Wife of General Custer*). Telephone interview, August 19, 2009.

Kortlander, Chris (director of Custer Battlefield Museum). Telephone
and correspondence February 16, 2010, March 25, 2010; in
person April 12, 2010; telephone and correspondence May 5,
2010, June 29, 2010.

MANUSCRIPT MATERIALS
Congressional Record, 44th Congress, 1st Session, Nos. 4627, 4628,
4629. National Archives.

Custer, Elizabeth. "Christmas on the Plains" (essay), AC2001-32 1872.
Montana Historical Society.

———. Letter to Mr. Fox, October 4, 1927. South Dakota State Historical
Society.

Custer, George. Letter to John M. Buckley, June 4, 1872. Burton
Historical Collection, Detroit Public Library, Detroit, Michigan.

Elizabeth Clift Bacon Journal, 1860–1863. C. W. Brice, Custer Collection
(private collection).

Elizabeth Custer Collection (private collection). Elizabeth Custer Library & Museum, Garryowen, Montana.

Elizabeth Custer Papers Collection: OGL #1496. Elwyn B. Robinson Department of Special Collections, Chester Fritz Library, University of North Dakota.

Frontier Fighters, Episode 24, June 26, 1926. Western Historical Manuscript Collection SL256, University of Missouri, St. Louis. Radio program.

Montana Historical Society. Elizabeth Custer Letter to Charles Woodruff, AC1952-2 1910.

Recruiting poster dated January 1, 1864, from Tecumseh, Michigan.

Reno, Marcus. *The Official Record of a Court of Inquiry Convened at Chicago, Illinois,* January 13, 1879.

Ronsheim, Milton. *The Life of a General (1929).* West Point Library Files, West Point, New York.

Thomas Weir Military Records & Personal Letters 1863–76. National Archives and Records Administration, M1064C:492.

Western Americana Collection / Elizabeth Custer Manuscript Collection. The Beinecke Rare Book and Manuscript Library, Yale University.

Western Americana Collection / George Custer Manuscript Collection. The Beinecke Rare Book and Manuscript Library, Yale University.

Williams, Rick. *Custer's Academy Years at West Point,* West Point Library Files, West Point.

INDEX

About the Authors

Howard Kazanjian, an award-winning producer and entertainment executive, has been producing feature films and television programs for more than thirty years. While vice president of production for Lucasfilm Ltd., he produced two of the highest-grossing films of all time, *Raiders of the Lost Ark* and *Star Wars: Return of the Jedi.* Some of his other notable credits include *The Rookie, Demolition Man,* and the first season of *JAG.*

In addition to his production experience, Kazanjian has worked closely with some of the finest directors in the history of cinema, including Alfred Hitchcock, Billy Wilder, Sam Peckinpah, Robert Wise, Joshua Logan, Clint Eastwood, George Lucas, Steven Spielberg, Elia Kazan, and Francis Ford Coppola. He is a longtime voting member of the Academy of Motion Picture Arts and Sciences, the Academy of Television Arts and Sciences, the Producers Guild of America, and the Directors Guild of America.

Chris Enss has been writing about women of the Old West for more than ten years. She loves Western culture and travels quite extensively, collecting research for her books. She received the Spirit of the West Alive award, cosponsored by the *Wild West Gazette,* celebrating her efforts to keep the

spirit of the Old West alive for future generations. She cur-
rently lives in a historic gold-mining town in Northern
California.